# SYNERGISTIC SELLING

## Grow Your Auto Sales, Inspire Top Producers And Dominate The Competition

Isn't it time to stop selling cars and
learn to help people buy them?
What I Have Learned from 9,000 Days
in the Retail Automobile Business

## Roger Williams

Nate Brown
"Deals aren't missed
by a few dollars
Deals ARE missed
by a few words"

Best

Published by Best Seller Publishing®, Pasadena, CA
Best Seller Publishing® is a registered trademark
Printed in the United States of America.
ISBN 153276247X

This publication is designed to provide accurate and authoritative information with regard to the subject matter covered. It is sold with the understanding that the publisher is not engaged in rendering legal, accounting, or other professional advice. If legal advice or other expert assistance is required, the services of a competent professional should be sought. The opinions expressed by the authors in this book are not endorsed by Best Seller Publishing® and are the sole responsibility of the author rendering the opinion.

Most Best Seller Publishing® titles are available at special quantity discounts for bulk purchases for sales promotions, premiums, fundraising, and educational use. Special versions or book excerpts can also be created to fit specific needs.

For more information, please write:
Best Seller Publishing®
1346 Walnut Street, #205
Pasadena, CA 91106
or call 1(626) 765 9750
Toll Free: 1(844) 850-3500
Visit us online at: www.BestSellerPublishing.org

# Table of Contents

# Foreword

Roger Williams has written a no-nonsense, real-world handbook for anyone wanting to take their best shot at reaching their fullest potential in the car business. You won't have to read for long to grasp that what's being presented can only be done by someone who:

- Has had a long-term, successful career in the automotive retail industry.
- Is still in that industry and continues to have a positive impact on it every day.
- Has remained fresh amidst a sea of industry change, and can thus deliver strategies that are fresh, relevant, and highly effective regardless of what you sell, or where you sell it.

Roger's book is filled with common-sense, moneymaking strategies that will benefit the veteran and newcomer to automotive sales alike. It's equally valuable to owners, managers, and sales professionals. Frankly, it should be required reading material for your entire team.

Synergistic Selling is not written just to be read, but to be studied, discussed at meetings, used as a training manual, and applied daily by everyone on your team.

I've known Roger Williams for three decades, and I can vouch for the fact that he walks his talk and is the "real deal." He has "been there and done that" better and longer than most, and now you'll have the profitable pleasure of discovering the same.

By the way, don't even think of reading this book without a highlighter and notepad handy. You don't go *through* a book like Synergistic Selling – you get *from* it.

Dave Anderson
President, LearnToLead

Foreword

# Acknowledgements

Thank you, Lori Williams; you are a true treasure from God. The spouses of salespeople are keys to success. Much like elevators, they can take you up or bring you down; Lori is my inspiration.

Special thanks to a great group of kids: Brooke, Jade, Trey, Laken, and Navy.

I'd also like to thank the following friends and career influences: Robert "Bobby" Crough, the greatest closer who ever lived. Dave Anderson, a rare friend and great mentor. The late Lynn Hickey, the greatest dealer who ever lived. The late Milton Moore, a true teacher of the auto business. The late Jimmy Head. Wade and Doug Hickey, Randall Hill, Curtis Franklin, Dale Early, James Davis, Raymond Palacios, Pat Gunning, Bill White, Frank and Chris Fletcher, Brent Lobanoff, Terry Walter and Jim Ziegler.

To the many salespeople I've worked with and/or trained, thank you all. Most of all, I'd like to thank all my customers.

# Acknowledgments

# Introduction

I started in the car business in my early 20s. Like many green salespeople before me, I wanted to revolutionize the business. I quickly realized that I never wanted to become like the old dinosaur salespeople who were constantly smoking, gambling, and pitching quarters – which they were all experts at. They were rude to the customers and rude to other people, and I didn't want to turn out like them.

Now, two and a half decades later, I have directed dealerships to record sales and profits many times over. I am revolutionizing the car business, one customer and one salesperson at a time. I have learned a lot, and I continue learning every day. And I pass forward what I have learned to others.

The three topics that are going to be the meat of this book are synergistic selling, modern technology, and coaching.

I learned about synergistic selling at Lynn Hickey Dodge, which was the first dealership I worked at. Synergistic selling is about how every little thing you do paints the big picture. It helped us sell 2,813 retail units in one month. We would have sold well over 3,000, but we simply ran out of inventory. At the end of the month, we had 23 acres of a mostly empty lot. We had sold over 2,000 retail units before, but 2,813 was the most ever. As a young man, I soaked up as much knowledge there as I could. I have since used this strategy to set sales records in numerous dealerships.

The second thing I will talk about is merging proven selling techniques with modern technology. There is a lot of information about ever-improving technology that we continually need to grasp. According to *Business Insider*, we sold approximately

18 million new cars in America in 2015.[1] That is the most ever, but we've continued to sell over 17 million per year. We just continue to grow.

But good times create bad habits, don't they? Inevitably, our techniques and skills suffer in good times. We have managers and salespeople who have been in the car business for only a few years who have no idea what recessions are about. They don't have the skillset that we needed in '07 and '08 when we had an economic crash to survive. They may have a hot product or a good location, and they are riding a wave, but they haven't created the wave. Low interest rates and big-time dealer cash incentives have created that wave.

The McKinsey report tells us that 10 years ago, the average consumer shopped at five dealerships before buying a car, and now that number is 1.6.[2] These days, many consumers do all their research online, and they narrow down what they want before they come to the lot.

Typically, when they come to our lot and meet our inexperienced salespeople and our inexperienced managers, we make it extremely difficult for them to spend their money to buy a car. To me, that is unacceptable.

One of my core beliefs has to do with the people process – coaching and developing people – which is the third main topic of this book. Coaching is about growing and adding value to your people. Without coaching, you are currently the best you will ever be. If you are going to make your own wave, you have to learn how to add value to your people.

---

[1]   DeBord, M. (2015, November 30). *Automakers are about to do something in the US that's never happened before*. Retrieved December 14, 2015, from http://www.businessinsider.com/automakers-are-about-to-do-something-in-the-us-thats-never-happened-before-2015-11

[2]   LeBeau, P. (2014, February 26). Americans rethinking how they buy cars. Retrieved January 13, 2016, from http://www.cnbc.com/2014/02/26/americans-rethinking-how-they-buy-cars.html

At the end of the day, good people with an average product will beat average people with a good product, and good people with an average process will beat average people with a good process. If you train your people to do their job well, you will beat the dealerships that have better selling products or better locations.

Growing and adding value to your people is paramount to separate the winners from the losers, the contenders from the pretenders. If you can train your salespeople and motivate them to learn the industry and become professionals, you will win, just as I have by using this strategy.

I believe in perpetual improvement, and that is something I train people to strive for. My training is unique. Most sales training is generic and performed by people who haven't sold cars successfully or managed dealerships to huge profits and big turnarounds. What they are good at is selling the dealers information they have learned from guys who actually work in dealerships. Very rarely do successful dealership turn-around specialists write books to disclose their knowledge, methods, and tips. But I get great joy from helping people, and I aim to shine the light and pass it forward.

The more skilled you are, the more value you bring to the dealership. Training has fallen by the wayside, so I feel called and compelled to share with you what I have learned and help you add value to your dealership.

I began writing this book over a decade ago, constantly adding and changing material. After 11 years in the making, I sincerely hope it will assist you in your sales career.

# Lessons from the Lot

Nearly nine thousand days on a car lot have taught me a thing or two – or 130.

1.  Teamwork makes the dream work.

2.  There is no telling what can be accomplished as long as no one cares who gets the credit.

3.  Car deals aren't missed by a few dollars; they are missed by a few words.

4.  If you don't have time to do it right the first time, when will you have time to do it right?

5.  Grow with the team; standing still is gradual separation.

6.  Take the deals on the 1$^{st}$ that you will take on the 31$^{st}$; they all count the same.

7.  Less than ordinary people get less than ordinary results. Ordinary people get ordinary results. Extraordinary people get extraordinary results. How can you be extraordinary?

8.  The first measure of insanity is doing the same thing again and again and expecting different results.

9.  If you continue to think the way you have always thought, you will continue to get what you always have got.

10. Become the change you wish to see.

11. Fix the person first, and the salesperson is an easy fix.

12. There are no normal deals; there are just deals.

13. FEAR – false events appearing real.

14. Discipline without direction is death.

15. The human mind is like a parachute; it only works when it's open.

16. When you are green, you are growing; when you are ripe, you are rotting.

17. Never get mad at your money.

18. Pride says, "It's impossible." Experience says, "It's risky." Reason says, "It's pointless." The heart whispers, "Give it a try."

19. Model yourself after successful people.

20. The more people you help get what they want, the more you will get what you want.

21. You don't get into the car business; the car business gets in you.

22. If you can't do great things, do small things in a great way.

23. Cars are much easier to replace than car deals.

24. Practice is the hardest part of learning, and training is the highway to success.

25. I'm thankful for the difficult people I have encountered in life; they have shown me who I don't want to be.

26. It doesn't take a thing of beauty to become a beautiful thing.

27. Proper preparation prevents poor performance.

28. Daily discipline done diligently determines destiny.

29. Stop waiting for what you want and start working with what you have.

30. If you think you can or think you can't, you are right.

31. If you can conceive it and believe it, you can achieve it!

32. There are no shortcuts when you are lost.

33. Always tell customers what you *can* do, never what you *can't* do.

34. There are only two *can'ts* in the sales business: If you can't sell you can't stay.

35. For every deal you miss by being too enthusiastic, you will miss 100 by not being enthusiastic enough.

36. Beautiful things happen when you separate yourself from negativity.

37. Hard work will beat talent when talent doesn't work hard.

38. There are two objections you will never overcome: ignorance and poverty.

39. The cure for all sales slumps is getting back to the basics.

40. Your attitude, not your aptitude, determines your altitude.

41. Writing down goals every day keeps failure away.

42. A goal without a plan is simply a wish.

43. Others may want to see you do good, but never better than them.

44. The difference between loser and closer is just a *C*; find your *C*!

45. Water seeks its own level regardless of where it is poured out.

46. In sales, you earn what you are worth.

47. Listen between the lines.

48. It's mind over matter; if you don't mind, it doesn't matter.

49. We are what we repeatedly do. Therefore, excellence is not an act but a habit.

50. The mark of an educated mind is to be able to entertain a thought without accepting it.

51. Success isn't final, and failure isn't fatal.

52. Things tend to work out best for those who make the best of how things work out.

53. Questions are the answer.

54. Two things you can control: your time and your attitude.

55. Figures lie and liars figure.

56. A manager with mediocre skills who inspires people will take you further than a highly skilled manager who inspires no one.

57. Good sales managers inspire themselves; great sales managers inspire others.

58. It takes big rocks, little rocks, gravel, and sand to fill a jar.

59. Those who cannot trust cannot *be* trusted.

60. To have a friend, you first have to be a friend.

61. Pigs get fat, and hogs get slaughtered.

62. Never let what you can't do stop you from doing what you can do.

63. A fish rots from the head down.

64. A smart person gives smart answers; a wise person asks smart questions.

65. If it is important to you, you will make time; if it's not important, you will make excuses.

66. Believe people when they show you who they are the first time.

67. We make a living by what we get, but we make a life by what we give.

68. Training is like showering: if not done daily you will begin to stink.

69. The only person you need to be better than is the person you were yesterday.

70. Fall in love with the process as much as you love the result, and your results will multiply.

71. What you think about all the time determines who you are and where you are going.

72. The best way to predict the future is to create it.

73. Positive thinking yields positive results.

74. If you can't admit anything is wrong, you won't change anything.

75. Complacency is the mother of mediocrity.

76. If you're not prioritizing your task, your day is managing you.

77. The greatest oak was once just a little nut that held its ground.

78. Success has 100 fathers, but failure is an orphan.

79. Leaders know, show, and go the way.

80. If you don't ask, the answer is always no.

81. Every job is a selfie of the person performing the work.

82. There are no failures, only experiences and your reaction to them.

83. Every manager is like an elevator: they take people up or bring them down.

84. No one cares how much you know until they know how much you care.

85. There are two things logic has nothing to do with, love and sales.

86. There are no elevators to success; you'll have to take the stairs.

87. You've got what it takes, but it will take everything you've got.

88. Good times create bad habits.

89. Shared grief is half the sorrow.

90. A lot of salespeople have talent, but few have championship habits.

91. You won't be able to stop the waves, but you can learn to surf!

92. Positive thinking allows you to do everything better than negative thinking.

93. You miss 100% of the shots you don't take.

94. Half of something beats all of nothing.

95. Everywhere you go, there you are.

96. Where there is no vision, the people perish (Proverbs 29:18, King James Bible).

97. He who hesitates is lost.

98. Sales are caught as much as they are taught.

99. The difference between success and significance: Success is about you, and significance is about others.

100. Life is not about waiting for the storm to pass; it's about learning to dance in the rain.

101. If serving is beneath you, leading is beyond you.

102. Pretend everyone has a sign around their neck that reads "Make me feel important."

103. People don't buy what you sell; they buy what you believe.

104. No one likes to be sold, but everyone likes to buy.

105. Nothing can be closed that isn't first opened. Be a good opener, and being a good closer is easy.

106. Trying to guess who the buyers are or what the buyers want is committing sales malpractice.

107. The bend in the road is only the end of the road if you don't turn.

108. Every day after work, we go home with a pocket full of money or a mouth full of excuses.

109. The difference between try and triumph is just a little *umph*.

110. Persistence overcomes resistance.

111. Some people look at things as they are and say, "Why?" I look at things as they could be and say, "Why not?"

112. Small people talk about people; average people talk about things; great people talk about ideas.

113. Fall in love with your work and you will be successful.

114. Telling isn't selling.

115. Yesterday is history, tomorrow is a mystery, today is the present – a gift; treat it as such!

116. Solid work, dedication, self-denial, living clean, and loving Jesus.

117. A happy person lives in a happy world an angry person lives in an angry world

118. Obstacles, problems, and other people can't stop you; only you can stop you.

119. Managers light a fire under people. Leaders light a fire inside people.

120. "What you do today can improve all your tomorrows."[3]

121. If you want to create greatness, stop asking for permission.

---

[3]     *Ralph Marston quote.* (n.d.). Retrieved December 18, 2015, from http://www.brainyquote.com/quotes/quotes/r/ralphmarst132966.html?src=t_motivational

122. Just when the caterpillar thought the world was ending, he turned into a butterfly.

123. Success is not final, failure isn't fatal, it is the courage to continue that matters

124. Opportunities don't happen; you create them.

125. Try not to be a person of success but a person of value.

126. I have not failed; I have found 1000 ways that do not work.

127. If you don't value your time, neither will others. Stop giving away your time and talents, and start charging for them.

128. Don't be afraid to give up the good for the great.

129. If you can't explain it simply, you don't know it well enough.

130. There is no shortage of people wanting to change their circumstances, but there's a shortage of people willing to change themselves.

131. Most men can stand adversity, if you wish to see the true character of a man, give him power.

CHAPTER 1

# Synergistic Selling

When I got into the car business back in the early '90s, I happened to start at one of the most successful car lots in history, called Lynn Hickey Dodge. It was owned by Lynn Hickey, who was a self-made man. Lynn and his sons Wade and Doug ran the dealership.

One day in a meeting, one of the managers mentioned something about synergistic selling. I asked the guys beside me, Tommy and Dallas, but they didn't know what that meant.

Then I asked the new car manager, David Milligan. Dave said: "It's a mixture of selling and energy." I wasn't sure he was sure, so I asked Milton Moore, who was my direct supervisor, and Milton said: "It's a whole bunch of little things that make a larger thing go."

Lynn was an innovator, and he was far ahead of his time. As he talked about setting sales records, doing things that had not been done before, and making plans for how we were going to do them, he had my full attention. Since I hadn't worked at any other car lot, I didn't realize how far advanced we were in the early '90s compared to all the other car lots. The things he did back then are still ahead of most dealers today.

Lynn had a lot of rules that I have learned and carried with me. Many people just focused on the negatives of what he did and never gave him credit for the many great things he did.

## Training Meetings

At Lynn Hickey Dodge, we had training meetings twice a day for 10 to 20 minutes at a time. Mandatory training everyday is unique to most dealers. Every morning at 8AM, Milton Moore held a meeting in the Dakota building. The other training session was held at noon. Milt trained from Jim Ziegler's sales manual among other tools.

If you were not on time for the meeting, you couldn't get in because the doors would be locked. You would also have to forfeit any spiff money from the previous day.

Spiff money was a way to incentivize the people working at the dealership. It was money that you would get above and beyond your normal commission. They could spiff you for anything – the biggest gross or lowest gross of the day. You never knew everything that would be spiffed, but old units were always spiffed. And you knew you would get a spiff all the time, especially on Saturdays.

As I said, if you were late for the training meetings, you would surrender your spiff money. It would go into a pot that the sales manager would spend on donuts or drinks. Sometimes they would take some of the money and buy something for everybody. Occasionally, Lynn even bought us B12 shots. Still, we wanted to make sure that we kept our spiff money, so almost all of us were on time for the meetings.

To win the title of salesperson of the month, you had to win what was known as the "Horse race," which was a unique blend of total sales, gross, and old-age units. Your units, front and back gross, and old-age units all gave you points. There was a lot of cash and recognition for being a productive sales person. It was always something imaginative and fun.

Each department – the wholesale lot (our onsite, buy-here-pay-here lot), the truck center, the used-car center, and the new-car center – would train their own people. Each department differed from the others.

In the training sessions, they would teach us all the things about selling cars that we might or might not know. They also shared all the ads we were running, what we had traded for, and what spiffs we had daily.

The meetings were never negative or focused on what we were doing wrong. The managers were not telling us about how great they had been when they sold cars. The sessions were always designed to add value to us to grow our skills and help us to become better salespeople. They were scheduled, planned, positive, and designed for a specific purpose: to create car-selling machines. And that is what they did. We were all very good because they trained us every day. We didn't have any choice. We had to learn. We knew all the ads we were running, and we knew what was expected of us in the Lynn Hickey sales process.

## The Liner-Closer System

A large factor was the liner-closer system. Regardless of your experience when you started at Lynn Hickey, you were put on a team.

Everybody started in a "liner-closer" system. In the liner-closer system, you would have up to 10 people on the team. If you were on the team as a salesperson, you had a team leader, who was a manager. The manager would get 20% of your commission in return for closing your deals, helping you learn how to follow up with your clients, and setting your appointments for you. This manager would manage you and teach you along the way.

If you sold up to eight cars, your commission was small. After eight cars, it got a little bigger. After 12 cars, it got bigger still. And so it continued, motivating you to sell more. After you sold 15 cars per month for 90 days, you could be a senior salesperson and be off the team, but you would not be a team leader, just a senior salesperson. Team leader was a great job. In that position, you could learn how to train people. It was also a way Lynn made sure that everybody did what he wanted to be done.

If you got in trouble for something, the managers wouldn't address it in public, so the customers or the other salespeople could see it. Instead, the managers would take you into their office. The whole setup was designed to keep things positive.

There was one main entrance at the Lynn Hickey Dodge dealership, but there were four smaller entrances to get in. You could get in a couple of places at the truck center, at the used-car lot, and at the Dakota building. However, there was only one exit. At each exit, there were spikes that would puncture your tires and a sign that said: "We are not responsible for tire damage. We are one of the biggest car lots in the world, and for insurance purposes, you must check out through the main entrance."

At the exit would be a salesperson dressed in a security guard uniform. This salesperson would look at the license plate or VIN (vehicle identification number) of the car and write it down. If it was our car, it had a barcode on it that the salesperson would scan. If some customers were leaving in their old car, the salesperson would say: "We're the biggest dealer in the world, and you're leaving in your car. What happened? How did we miss you?"

The security guard, a.k.a. the salesperson, had a radio on hand. If he or she turned around the customers at the gate and we sold them a car, this salesperson could make between $100 and $500. You wanted to be the security guard because then you got to turn everybody around all day long. It was a very well-paying job because most people would turn around.

In the car business, "T.O." is common lingo, and stands for turnover. You turn customers over to a manager when all progress stops, and you are unable to sell them a car.

Lynn believed in having several turns on the deals. He wanted several managers to talk to people. Lo and behold, it worked. The liner-closer system combined with the turnaround at the gate set everything up for a fast pace.

When you closed deals with customers and got them ready to go into financing, you turned them over to what was called the "touch team." The touch team was a team of girls who were

SYNERGISTIC SELLING   Roger Williams

product specialists. They knew everything about the cars, and they would do the deliveries. You would turn the customers over to that team as soon as the deal was closed and the offer to purchase was signed. Then you would go out to the car lot and get what in the car business is known as another "up" – a new customer. You would start the process with this new customer while the touch team delivered your car.

## Pager Systems

Another thing that was unique about Lynn Hickey was that he issued pagers, which was the quickest form of communication in those days. I was a young man who had never been to other car lots, so I didn't realize that other dealers didn't issue pagers.

The pagers were the type that you could put a note on. All the receptionists knew how to page you. For example, they could page you and say: "Roger Williams, your customer, Jonathan, is up on new cars." Or they could say: "There is a meeting for this or that," or "Conversion vans at $1,000 mini.," meaning if you sold a conversion van, you made $1,000 minimum commission. This was the type of information they would give over your pager. Your pager was always going off, so you always knew what was going on.

Depending on the time of year, we had between 120 and 200 plus salespeople at the dealership. In addition, we had about 30 to 50 managers, counting finance managers and team leaders. All these managers had to page about someone who bought a car every couple of hours, and it was announced over the loud speakers. So about every couple of minutes or so, there would be a page going on.

The pages would start with "Flags are flying, and people are buying," "Banners are waving, and people are saving," or "Balloons are flying, and people are buying." So, for example, it would go: "Flags are flying, people are buying, and we just sooold another one. Lynn Hickey Dodge and Roger Williams would like to thank Adam and Deborah Archer on their purchase of a 1994

Dodge Caravan. Mr. and Mrs. Archer, thank you for shopping at the world's Number 1 volume dealer, Lynn Hickey Dodge." We paged every real customer, but most of the time, the pages were names we made up just to excite the public, and it worked. All the customers who came in would say: "Gosh, you guys sure are selling a lot of cars."

## Marketing

The Hickey's marketing was also ahead of the times. Our TV and radio commercials sounded like they happened in real time. A lot of them were conversations between two people. We had a guy named Tom Parks, who would say, "Tomorrow, Monday" for a commercial that would be aired on a Sunday. On commercials that would air on a Tuesday, he would say, "Today, Tuesday," and so on. That way, it would seem like he was right there at whatever big sale was going on. He would talk about the sale, and he would always have the lowest interest rate possible and a very low payment and price on new and used cars.

Lynn even got Evel Knievel to come to the dealership. They filmed a commercial where Evel Knievel, together with Lynn and Tom, got up in a crane that held a Dodge Van. Then Lynn shot a bazooka at a Chevy truck, which was the most popular truck in Oklahoma at that time. The Chevy truck blew up, and we started "Countdown 3,000." It signalized our attempt at selling 3,000 units in one month. Is also signalized that the new Dodge trucks were here. Dodge had had a similar truck from '72 to '93, but the '94 trucks were a total makeover, so it was a big deal, and we had hundreds of them. We even had our own truck center separate from the other facilities.

## Business Development Center

Before anybody else I know of had one, we had a business development center (BDC for short) where we would take the incoming calls and make outgoing calls to set appointments. I was quite negative about it, thinking: "Gosh, I'm pretty successful at this. Why would I need a bunch of girls in the office to make calls for me and take the incoming phone calls? They're going to cut me off." I went to Milton, and I complained about it. He told me to calm down and relax. "We'll see how this works," he said.

Sure enough, the girls were much better on the phone than most of the salespeople, and they were setting a lot of appointments. We had an appointment culture where we would have 25 to 50 appointments on the board for most weekdays and often hundreds of appointments on weekends. Pretty soon, I was buying appointments from the girls, even though we weren't supposed to.

Every customer who came to the lot was registered to win a big TV from a drawing, and all the customer information was given to the BDC. They followed up and set appointments with this information.

Most dealers today still haven't caught on to this appointment culture. They don't understand that if you call customers and set appointments, the customers will come in, and you will sell more cars.

## The Look and Feel

Everything about the dealership was designed to make it easy for the customers. It was plainly painted to indicate which way they should go when they drove into the lot. We would valet park for them, and then we would take them on a golf cart, or we would walk with them, depending on what they wanted to see.

Lynn would drive around his lot to ensure that it looked appealing from all angles. Red is a color that attracts people, and Dodge dealerships are supposed to be red. Lynn had a lot of red at his dealership as well. Then the inside of the buildings were painted with earth tones that were supposed to relax people. Everything from how the entrance was designed to how the buildings were painted was done to sell more vehicles. The cars were always straight, and the grass was always manicured and kept perfect. It was very powerful to the minds of the salespeople and the customers.

Every car in the dealership had to have a balloon on it at all times. If Lynn drove in, and the cars didn't have balloons on them, it wasn't very long before we had new porters and new salespeople who would put on balloons.

Lynn also had music playing over the speakers all the time. So when we did our pages: "The flags are flying, people are buying," we cut into the music. Everything we did was designed to create enthusiasm and sell cars.

In addition, we always had a large inventory. Some dealers turn down factory allocated cars, but we didn't turn down cars from the factory. The Hickey philosophy was that there is a butt for every seat. When we had meetings, Lynn would say: "If your mind can conceive it, and you can believe it, then you can achieve it." He believed that. He didn't see a reason he couldn't outsell every dealership in the world from a stand-alone Dodge dealership in Oklahoma City. So we did. (A stand-alone dealership means that it's just one dealership. It wasn't a Dodge, Chrysler and Jeep; it was just a Dodge store.)

There was a system for everything from how you met the customers and what you said to them all the way through the appraisals and deliveries. Respecting the customers' time was of high importance. The managers walked around saying "Hello" and shaking hands. It was all designed to facilitate the sale of a vehicle. The Hickeys had a synergistic approach to the training, the BDC, the pay plan, and the motivation.

In June of 1994, Lynn Hickey Dodge sold and retailed 2,813 new and used vehicles. That is still a world record as far as I know at a stand-alone dealership. So to retail 2,813 vehicles was incredible. Lynn, Wade, and Doug made a plan for it, and we executed it.

Lynn died a few years ago,[4] and I went to his funeral. He was a big influence on my life. Bob Crough (pronounced *crow*) once told me: "Managers build fires under people. Leaders build fires inside people." Lynn was a leader who lit fires inside people, and he lit a fire inside me.

Few dealers today focus on synergistic selling. They exhaust their customers, salespeople, and managers with all the hoops they make them jump through to buy a car. They lack an understanding of how to drive their high achievers to want to sell more so they can earn more. They also lack an understanding of how important it is to have a large inventory for the customers to choose from. The small amount they save on floor plan interest pales compared to the amount they lose on missed sales.

The way that Lynn ran his dealership was ingenious and ahead of its time, and I carry it with me. Over the years, I have gotten a good reputation as a dealership turnaround specialist – a guy who can come into a dealership and make it become more profitable in a short period of time. Much of my success can be attributed to implementing many of the synergyistic strategies that I learned from Lynn Hickey.

Often dealers try to limit our success, saying "You can't do this, and you can't do that." Everyone who owns a dealership has little idiosyncrasies. But whichever Lynn Hickey-style strategies they allow me to implement, I do, and I am always successful at turning around or improving a dealership. Thus far in various markets with all different manufacturers' I'm 100% in my turn around attempts.

I'd be remiss if I didn't mention a few of the guys who get it.

Frank Fletcher has 12 dealerships in Missouri and Arkansas. He has a unique pricing strategy where he puts large commissions and low prices on "hit list" and "green tag" units. This prevents taking

---

4   *Lynn Hickey, former Oklahoma City Dodge dealer, dies.* (2012, December 28).
    Retrieved November 23, 2015, from http://www.autonews.com/article/20121228/
    RETAIL07/121229924/lynn-hickey-former-oklahoma-city-dodge-dealer-dies

auction losses on pre-owned units and helps move new units out more quickly. Frank does a "window pricing" strategy on all his units that has worked well for him. He possesses the diligence to personally price each trade-in from the 12 different dealerships!

Another unique thing he does is he personally decides if his dealerships wholesale or retail a trade-in the day after the trade is received. This prevents managers from loading up in trades that are not worth the money. Frank has taken a lifelong passion for cars and made it into a very successful dealership chain. Frank is a friend and a mentor to me and I enjoy working with him.

Pat Gunning, owner of G&A Marketing, puts a lot of synergistic excitement in his events. Taping off the lot, the hanging tags, and the balloons – His events are designed to create excitement. I thoroughly enjoyed working with him. Unfortunately, so many people have started staffed event companies and most of them are people who can't make it at a dealership or people you don't want at your dealership. Pat does it right and understands the synergistic philosophy.

Neil Alderman owner of The Synergy Group Neil will send a coach to your store for three days, a coach that is an expert and appointment setter. This teaches your sales associates to be successful when there is no trainer in town. Neil is an industry leader known for driving traffic with his six phase digital/direct mail media blitz. If you want to drive more traffic you can reach him through my website AutoMotiveCoach.net

These guys all have different business models, but each is very successful.

CHAPTER 2

# Selling in the Greatest Time of All

Last month, I had my very first Uber ride. I was doing some training in Little Rock, Arkansas, and that evening, a friend booked me an Uber ride to take me back to my hotel after a social gathering.

In a matter of minutes, a gentleman in a Prius pulled up. We exchanged pleasantries, and he told me about his job. He described himself as a tech nerd, and his job was making apps for cellular devices, computers, laptops, and so on. Then he asked me what I did.

"I'm a professional automobile retailer," I told him.

"A car salesman," he said almost sarcastically.

"Yes," I replied, "it boils down to that. I teach, coach, and manage car salespeople, but I still get my share of interaction with customers."

"Teach and coach salespeople?" He asked incredulously.

"I'm a speaker, teacher, writer, and trainer of salespeople. I've taught thousands over the years. I get joy from teaching people how to be the best at what they do," I replied.

He paused, pondering his next question, and then he finally asked: "How about today's Internet and information age – the access that people have to so much information – how are you dealing with that?"

I could easily ascertain that he was strongly angling for the answer he wanted, something like: "Yes, the Internet and transparency have hurt the business, and I don't know how we will survive."

Instead, I told him the rather shocking truth, which seemed to be difficult for him to swallow. I said: "Yes, it has changed things, and I absolutely love it. I wish we had always had it. It's the greatest tool for our industry in my lifetime."

I could tell my answer surprised him, and I continued: "The real information is the best part. We car salespeople are thrilled that customers now have real information from someone besides us. We have a large group of dealerships, and this year, we have had our best first quarter ever, following up our record year in auto sales last year, when 18 million new units were delivered in the U.S."

He paused again. Not getting the answer he expected, he pressed on hoping for an answer he wanted to hear. Initially stuttering, he went on: "W-what about all the pricing information, the transparency of viewing and comparing so many dealers' prices, and arming yourself with knowledge from your home? It has to be a lot tougher for you guys to do what you do with such an informed and well-equipped customer? I mean c'mon, knowledge is power."

At this point, I laughed out loud: "Buddy, you just named many of the reasons why I love the information age so much." I continued: "Suppose you felt you had received a bad rap, and your industry had a lot of misinformation and bad information spewed and spread about it from sources that had a self-serving agenda. Then wouldn't the information age be a breath of fresh air to you?

Now the lion's share of media scare tactics and myths have been exposed thanks to the wonder of modern technology. If a salesperson says: 'All dealers have virtually identical invoices, and this model has only $300 markup,' years ago, the customers would have to shop four or five dealerships to find out if this was true. I mean, who are customers more likely to believe: salespeople or their own research? It is wonderful that our customers are so much more educated than before.

Without all the misinformation out there, we don't get as many ridiculously low offers or absurd trade value demands. Also, people no longer shop at five dealerships, threaten to shop in another town where they mistakenly believe cars are cheaper, or become angry or upset because they don't understand something, and so on.

These last few years have been record years for some carmakers as well as many dealerships, including ours. The information age has turned on the light, and the cockroaches have run into the darkness. Many car dealers now have proof that what we have been saying all along is true."

Then he asked: "Aren't your margins significantly smaller than they used to be?"

I answered: "The Internet has educated our customers to the extent that the people who sell 'fear the dealer' to customers are having a tougher go of it. Many realize they get 'ripped off' for more money on their insurance policies, cell phones, burial expenses, utility bills, and clothing than on the average 4% to 8% markup at a dealership.

You are correct that our margins are slightly smaller, but not significantly. They are almost parallel to our average markup decrease. And with more manufacturers paying out record volumes of bonus money, the margins per unit will naturally tighten up."

This stunned him. He stuttered a bit, and then asked: "H-h-how about all the dealer add-ons from the finance guys – you know, the warranties, gap policies, and all of that nonsense and junk you don't need?"

I replied: "I'm the corporate sales manager of 12 dealerships, and I've done this over 25 years. I've stood in the service lane with families crying because of their circumstances. Say they have an 80,000-mile Toyota Sienna mini-van, and the transmission is out, but it's out of warranty. Then it's going to be $4,500 to fix it, but they can't afford it. They don't have a credit card to put it on either, but they can't leave with their vehicle because it won't drive. Since they can't afford to fix it, they are standing in my service lane crying. A $25- or $30-a-month service contract would have paid for that. I guess you are the type of person who would advise them that that's junk they don't need."

Insurance companies also sell warranties. "If you don't think a warranty is something worth having, you are not obliged to buy one, but in situations where it makes sense to protect your investment, it's better to be safe than sorry protecting an investment. Is sound advice".

I decided to have a little fun, so I posed a question: "If I gave you $2,000 today, would you agree to pay for all repairs of every breakdown of my current model SUV for the next seven years or 120,000 miles, including towing, rental car, and hotel allowances? Oh, and give me back a pro-rated portion if I trade, sell, or total it?"

There was quite a long pause as if he didn't understand the question. Then he said: "Well when you say it like that..."

I said, "You mean reversing the roles?" I continued: "The Internet has educated our customers. They know that insuring their investments is sound financial advice. Many people, myself included, enjoy the peace of mind knowing we are insured for the rising cost of auto parts and repair. Informed customers weigh the value versus the cost of extended warranties and make decisions based on the individual facts of their purchase."

The driver was not happy with the education he was receiving. He quickly snapped: "Yeah, but the customers don't need any of that. They could buy good cars."

I asked: "So hoping to buy only good vehicles that never need repair is a much better plan than purchasing protection? If hoping is more beneficial than insuring to you, then by all means, purchase as little insurance as possible. It is my experience that over insuring beats under insuring. It's also my experience that everyone makes good cars these days. However, the cars are made of thousands of parts, mostly moving or attached to moving parts, and none are guaranteed beyond the factory warranty."

Then he asked me if we also sell gap insurance. I told him that we do, and I continued: "Anybody who borrows more than their car is worth needs gap insurance because if their car gets stolen, totaled, or whatever, and it isn't worth as much as they owe on it, they are stuck with that additional payoff money on it, and they have to roll over to another car to pay it.

I think technology has assisted customers in understanding the need for a service contract to cover them for the life of the loan or longer. And I believe that they understand gap insurance more. When we have to offer them the base payment without anything extra, most customers already know that they also want a warranty for however long they plan on keeping the car. So it has helped that guy in the finance office a lot as well.

People can also shop their own rates these days, so if we can meet or beat their rates, we typically earn their finance business. It has been very beneficial all the way around."

As the driver sat there pondering, I continued enlightening him: "You see, some people perpetuate the belief that education is worthless or that teachers, cops, and priests are all bad. But the Internet has been extremely useful in dispelling old scare tactics, exposing the tall tales, and shining a light on the devaluation of individuals, businesses, and goods. The Internet has exposed the people who could once hide while villainizing others. I firmly believe the Internet is the greatest tool the auto industry has ever known. I can't even begin to get into the advertising advantages or the customer retention management aspect."

At about that time, we arrived at my hotel, and he said: "I can tell you're a really good salesman, but I'm going to fact check our conversation. No offense meant," he added.

I said: "By all means, research how many new and pre-owned cars dealers are selling, and notice that our profit margins are not significantly dropping. And check to see if Warren Buffett's Berkshire Hathaway just invested several billion dollars in auto dealerships and if Warren was quoted as saying he was going to buy more.

I apologize I couldn't dispel your notion that the Internet had somehow harmed, exposed, or crippled us car dealers, or that getting information to customers has hindered us in any way. But please accept my most sincere gratitude for computer geeks like you for making it possible for us to have our greatest information and advertising tool ever! I mean that; thank you so much!"

## Some Fabulous Facts

Again this year I predict U.S. Sales over 18 million new cars and light trucks – that is, pickups, SUVs, crossovers and minivans. [...] breaking the record set in 2015. However, U.S. auto sales had a long way to climb, after falling to only 10.4 million in 2009. Analysts said that was the lowest level of U.S. auto sales per capita since World War II.[5]

As I said before, the McKinsey report tells us that 10 years ago, the average consumer shopped at five dealerships before buying a car, but now that number has dropped to 1.6.[6] These days, many consumers have done all their research online. They know what they want, and they understand the packages better. They are so well informed that it helps us deliver when they come to the dealership.

Three-fourths of all the customers who come into the car lot these days have been to the Internet first. They have looked at the packages, colors, and options that they want. They have also figured out what fits in their budget.

In the past, we used to ask them to trust us. Of course, they didn't. We were car salespeople; we were somewhere lower than politicians, lawyers, and criminals. Now they come to the lots, and they know that what we tell them is the truth.

---

[5]   http://www.detroitnews.com/story/business/autos/2015/11/17/new-car-sales/75938626/

[6]   LeBeau, P. (2014, February 26). Americans rethinking how they buy cars. Retrieved January 13, 2016, from http://www.cnbc.com/2014/02/26/americans-rethinking-how-they-buy-cars.html

There are very few false expectations anymore. Before, people used to get their trade valued by their banker. They could come in and say: "My old trade is worth $20,000 because that's what my banker said." What they perhaps didn't say was that their banker had said so two years earlier. Now it's live time. People log on, put in the miles and the VIN number of their car, and get a real appraisal. It has cleared out a lot of falsehoods, and it has helped us to create a bond with our customers that makes the transaction faster and easier. That is why so many more people are trading.

Also, the fear is gone. It has taken out the fear for the customers because they can go online and feel comfortable with the information they get. It has taken out the fear for the salespeople because they don't have to explain to their customers what their trade is worth. The customers have gone online, and they have seen that.

The only people who still believe auto dealerships have huge markups and certain cities or dealers have vast savings on cars are people who do not have access to the Internet or have reading comprehension issues.

One complaint I hear from more and more customers using third party car-buying sites is: "I could have walked in and bought it myself, because with the small markup the rebate is the only discount I got." Especially many smaller cars, regardless of manufacturer, have no more than $200 or $300 between MSRP and invoice.

## Marketing to the Masses Has Become Much Easier

Thirty years ago, dealers would have given their right arm to be able to contact their customers in real time and tell them everything about their dealership through e-mail or by sending them to their website.

The old-fashioned way of advertising was to sit down and draw up newspaper ads for hours at a time and compare other people's ads. The poor old newspaper, once the king of car ads, is virtually dead. Now that all newspapers are online, they are pushing through social media sites and other websites designed to capture the attention of the smartphone web browsers.

In the 1990s and early 2000s, direct mail was the bomb. Dealers sent out mailers that got progressively larger, glossier, and thicker to persuade the customers into thinking they had won a grand prize rather than a door prize, just to get them in the door. Why did direct mail have to get so blatantly ridiculous? You guessed it: Snail mail got passed up by the technology era. Now, dealerships and marketing companies that are experts in using direct mail sales to generate traffic are struggling to drive traffic with it. It just doesn't work like it used to.

How about TV? Like direct mail, advertising on TV no longer works like it used to. It has become so inefficient that now our ads are often tied to the stations' social media and websites. The social media and website tie-ins are the TV stations' effort to hold on to their advertising dollars. The cheesy commercials are worthless. Pros like Tom Parks were once the kings of driving traffic. For several decades, they masterfully pitched the dealers they worked for. But there have been fewer and fewer results per dollar spent on TV in recent years; the ROI has not been there.

How about radio? It still hangs in there, better than TV in most markets. And like TV, it's often tied to social media or Internet websites operated by the station and their affiliates. But it's just not as powerful a medium as it used to be. The radio message works best when the talent is a dealer or manager who is well known and has local celebrity status, or the ad is very strong in content. With satellite radio, podcasts, smartphone music downloads, etc., the radio has suffered a steady decline in dealer ROI as well.

The news is not all bad. In fact, it's much more positive than negative. Technology and the World Wide Web have opened great doors of communication with our customers. Now we can communicate live time with our customers through texts, email, and videos. Google, Facebook, Bing, YouTube, and a growing list of websites owned by lead generators are now at our disposal. Third-party lead generation sites are already getting squeezed out, many being swallowed by the manufacturers and dealers. Even the larger Dealer Management System providers are buying the third party generators and providers.

Now, people can pull up the inventory of dealers from Los Angeles to New York City with just a few taps on their cell phones. They can get a lot of information, and we are able to reach them very easily. It has restored a bond between the consumer and the auto industry that people thought would never be repaired.

Some dealers run from the Internet because they have the same thought process as the Uber driver I had; they think the Internet will somehow expose or hurt them. But what they don't realize is that it's their greatest tool.

Rather than comparing newspaper ads or film cheesy TV commercials, today's dealers had better be busy viewing all of their inventory online and comparing their sites to their competitors' sites, looking at how every other dealer has their units marketed, and how they are priced!

In today's digitally connected world, it is imperative that businesses take control of their social media and online reputation in order to succeed.

> 75% of car buyers [...] say Internet research, including
> social media and review sites, was the most helpful
> medium when selecting a car dealership – surpassing all
> other mediums. [7]

This is something dealerships cannot ignore.

We speak with our customers in a virtual world every day! Our clients see our smiling sales associates and converse with them

---

[7]    Digital Air Strike Releases 2015 Social Media Trends Study for the Automotive
     Industry. (2015, November 3). *Dealer Marketing*. Retrieved December 14, 2015,
     from http://www.dealermarketing.com/digital-air-strike-releases-2015-social-
     media-trends-study-for-the-automotive-industry/

from the convenience of their home or car. Auto sales are in their greatest age ever. The information age has taken the old myths and tall tales out of the equation. The transparency of the business does not work against us; it works in our favor.

Another advantage of the information age is that it has allowed us to improve our training. Instead of waiting for training books to come in the mail, all of our salespeople can get online and learn everything about the new cars that are coming. There are many online training sites. I'm prejudiced, but I believe AutomotiveCoach. net is the best value and most useful one.

The Internet also allows us to look at everybody else's pricing strategies. We can look at the auction value of the cars. We used to have to wait for it to come in the mail, but now we just make a few clicks to see what all the cars are bringing at auction.

The transparency and speed of communication have created a lot more comfort for sales staff, sales managers, and consumers.

If dealers in today's time of technology, transparency, and communication are not taking advantage of the Internet and using it as their advocate, they are going to be extinct very soon. The Internet is the present and the future, and it makes you or breaks you. It's the greatest tool in the history of automobile sales, and not to use the greatest tool available is very unwise.

If you ignore or only half-heartedly embrace the Internet, you will get the exact results you deserve. No tool, regardless of its strength, can be effective when it is not understood or used.

The famous Seminole warrior Coacoochie, a.k.a. "Wildcat," known for his fearlessness as well as his eloquence, referenced technology during his surrender:

The whites are, I know, too strong for us. [...] You can make powder; I cannot. [...] I care little for myself. [...] Hunger cannot wet the eyes of a brave man, or embitter his proud heart, [...] but my women, my children suffering.[8]

This is exactly the stance many dealers need to embrace. The powder that Wildcat referred to was gunpowder. For dealers, the powder is the Internet. Stubborn dealers may stick with conventional media and leave the Internet in the hands of others who self-monitor or are not monitored or held accountable by the sales managers. These dealers will watch their dealership suffer.

All dealers everywhere are wanting more traffic. I have the strategies, and solutions. I do it everyday. Log on to AutoMotiveCoach.Net and schedule your live event training session. I show you how to drive traffic and how to turn that traffic into sales.

---

[8]     Stone, S. (2003, October 30). *Coacoochee - Seminole War Chief.* Retrieved December 14, 2015, from http://freepages.genealogy.rootsweb.ancestry. com/~crackerbarrel/Coacoochee.html

# CHAPTER 3

# Technology: It Will Make or Break You; It's Your Choice

In this chapter, I will discuss how you can marry modern technology with old-school sales techniques that are proven to yield excellent results. Great technology without salesmanship is useless.

A lot of people think they have to make a choice between old school and new school technology. However, I believe that before you burn that old school down, you probably should get the math book, the science book, the psychology book, the English book, and the geometry book out of there. Let's make sure that we still do basic math and English, and that we don't limit ourselves to modern technology.

## Customer Retention Management

First I want to talk about the Customer Retention Management tool or CRM. CRM is something every dealership that I know has. It used to be a manual sales log that people would write in. It would include a quick description of the customers, the name of the salesperson who helped them, the name of the car this person showed the customers, the step of the sale they got to, whether or not the customers were turned over to a manager, and whether or not the customers bought the car. Now that every dealership has a CRM, the salespeople have to put all the information that we used to write in the sales log into the CRM.

Strangely and miraculously, when dealerships began using CRM, and they got rid of their manual sales logs, their closing percentage skyrocketed, but their traffic slowed down a considerable amount. The reason was that the salespeople didn't put every customer's information into the CRM.

When your customers' information is not put into the CRM, you don't know if the advertising mediums you use are working. You don't know how much traffic is coming to your store. You don't know what ad you ran that brought them in. You don't know how to manage your store because you don't have the traffic numbers. You don't know which cars they ask for. You can't send them letters if you do a direct mail sale. You can't email them if you do an email blast. You can't call them or text them because you don't have any information on them since the salespeople did not enter them into the CRM.

I travel to a lot of stores, and when the managers are not present, I ask the salespeople: "Hey, what percentage of your ups (customers) make it into the CRM?" Typically they are honest with me, and they tell me some numbers. Some are around 50%. That is an alarming number if you are a dealer or a general manager, and you are spending your money to get people to the dealership.

The sales managers, who are responsible for making sure that the salespeople put the customers in the CRM, think the salespeople put everybody in the CRM, but that is not true, and it never has been true. Just a few years ago, the dealerships trusted that the salespeople would fill out the manual log whenever they had customers. They never did. In the same way, they won't put all their customers into the CRM just because you have it.

CRM works against you, not for you, if you don't monitor it and make sure all the information is put into it. Like I said, if the information is not in the system, you can't contact those customers, and you don't know what advertising is working.

A well-run dealership has a sales log that is kept by a manager or receptionist. It doesn't have to be a paper sales log; the manager or receptionist could also use the CRM. Whoever is responsible for the CRM logs the customer encounters they observe. Then the salespeople have to come back and fill it out.

If you don't inspect what you expect on your CRM and your monitoring of your traffic, you are only going to monitor the traffic that the salespeople want you to know about, so you have to have a manager or receptionist whose function is to monitor and make sure the customers are put into the log.

I have hired two receptionists before, one to answer the phone and the other to do CRM and some other tasks. Sometimes, I have even hired what I call an "up-counter," and that person monitors the logs. It's amazing how much more traffic you have when people are paid to monitor it.

You can't trust your salespeople to enter every customer into the CRM. If you do, you are not running your store properly, and you are missing many customers. They fall into what I call a technology hole.

As useful as the CRM tool is, it is only as effective as the people who enter the information into it. Leaving the CRM in the sales associates' hands has been and always will be trouble. Much like our old handwritten logs were only effective when managers, rather than salespeople, logged the customers, the old fashioned way of having a manager in charge of accounting for the CRM entries and updates is the only way to make it work.

What about your "virtual ups" – are those tracked? Virtual ups are what I call everybody who has emailed or called the store asking questions after going to your website. These must be tracked and followed up with.

Does your website sell? If you were to walk customers up to your website, and you were not allowed to speak--you could just move the mouse around and click buttons-- would you be able to sell to your customers? Would they see what special interest rates you have? Would they see what has 0% on it, or what has huge discounts on it? Would they be able to learn about what big sale you are having through the manufacturer, your credit unions, captive lenders, or whatever? If your website doesn't sell, you could be in trouble.

Sales managers particularly seem to despise tracking the opportunities. They despise it because it's tedious, and it's cumbersome. It requires constant attention. It's just not fun to monitor the lot and real and virtual traffic, but it must be done.

Everybody who emails you, everybody who calls you, everybody who comes into the store, and everybody who shows up at your car lot must be entered into your CRM.

## New Manager Responsibilities and Roles

As we are ushering in a new era of technology, we are also ushering in a new era of manager responsibilities and manager roles.

The managers have to know how many emails come to the store, how many people call the store, how many people visit the store, and how many people come to the service department, all on a daily basis. They also need to know the appointment percentage, how many are shows and no-shows, and the closing percent on emails and calls.

Sales managers must treat every opportunity as if it's a guest in their physical showroom. Each email, call, and contact must be tracked, charted, and followed up with by the sales managers every day in the CRM. Your true traffic count now is the people who come to your lot physically and your virtual contact.

Good stores typically record incoming phone calls so they can be monitored. All dealers I know who think they have great people are surprised when they listen to the recordings of their people on incoming phone calls. They are shocked by the poor job that they do.

You have to monitor everything you want to improve. If you can't monitor it, how can you improve it? If you don't know how many appointments you had, how are you going to improve your appointment percentage? If you don't know how many appointments you had who didn't show, how are you going to improve that? If you don't know how many appointments are being set per phone call or email, how are you going to improve that?

The new technology has led us to have an appointment culture. The customers do a lot of the work online by looking at the different packages, learning what they cost, and finding out what their trade-ins are worth. So, when they contact us, we can't wait for the next day or two days, and we can't have some automatic responder responding to them. It has to be live time, and the managers have to get involved.

Many dealerships have separate business development centers (BDC) and sales teams with little manager interaction with BDC. This is not effective, and you must integrate the sales managers and BDC into one team. The managers have to be actively involved in both the BDC process and the e-commerce process. The managers should be answering the emails and taking phone calls, and they should be taking turnovers via email, text messages, and phone calls. The BDC's assigning leads only to sales people is a weak and ineffective method. Each lead must be assigned to a manager and a sales associate.

If you use a different computer system in your BDC than your normal CRM, you need to make sure that you integrate those, and assign each opportunity to a manager and a sales associate. That way, all the sales managers can log onto their CRM and know everything that is happening. Then they can be aware of what is currently going on in their dealership. They can know about the emails that are coming in, what they say, and what the response is. They can know what stock number somebody is interested in. They can know how many miles away a phone call came from. If somebody calls you from more than 30 minutes away, you had better get it right because you are not going to have a second chance. They have to pass by dealerships to get to you. The managers have to know and manage these things. They can't just leave it to the

BDC anymore. If they do, they need to be fired, and you need to get some new managers who manage by talking to the customers and setting appointments themselves.

Many managers are not managing the BDC or the e-commerce. They are just trying to manage the live showroom floor, and they are not even managing that because they are letting the salespeople put the customers into the CRM. They are just submitting deals and waiting for the salespeople to bring them another deal. Those who do that are pseudo-managers. They are faking being managers, and they are not managing anything.

When you get an email, your BDC or whoever is in your Internet department should log that email into CRM and then reply to this email immediately so that the sales manager at the sales desk can see this email and reply. As soon as a phone call comes in, it too should be logged in the CRM. It needs to be in the CRM so that the sales managers and the Internet team can discuss every deal as it happens. That is why the sales managers have to make themselves available and be on CRM with the BDC or the Internet team. They can't say, "Just get them in." They have to take turnovers on the phone and email. They have to be proficient at it themselves. They have to help monitor what is going on, and they have to get involved in the traffic generated on the virtual showroom floor, which are the website, emails, and phone calls. It's vital that managers manage the BDC and the e-commerce – the virtual showroom. They must manage *all* the leads, and they must be the ones who price the cars.

*Every* general manager and dealer should know everything about their website, Internet advertising, and e-commerce. The sales manager and the Internet manager should be the same.

A culture is never finished; you can develop it continually. Your managers need to be able to combine the old-fashioned role of managing the salespeople and the customers who physically come to the sales floor, with the new roles of managing the virtual showroom.

Managers who are incapable of helping you in the modern technology era won't lead you into the future. And you will miss out on sales if you have managers who do not understand the technology and are unwilling to learn it. The sales skills necessary for a high closing percentage and elevated grosses while working with live customers are similar to those needed for virtual customers, but not exactly the same. Without adapting modern selling techniques to the modern buyer, the methods of the 90s and early 2000s are not going to propel you anywhere but down.

## Finding the Right Balance

In the mid-'90s, we were told that the Internet would immediately take over the world. So we all opened Internet departments. They didn't fare so well in the initial years. Every somewhat techy salesperson who wasn't very good at sales but we liked and didn't want to fire for lack of production, became the Internet manager. They typically didn't sell a lot of cars, but they could fix the dealerships' computers when they went down. Now the Internet department is a life blood of our dealerships. Soon this will evolve into managers taking customers "cradle to grave". Setting the appointment, working the deal, and contracting the purchase.

Now there are as many people working in the Internet department as on the regular showroom floor, and you must have well-trained salespeople there.

The Internet is a great tool for car dealers, but you have to know how to use it. The technology is only as good as you make it. The two biggest mistakes you can make are ignoring the modern technology or being overly dependent on it.

If you ignore modern technology, you have no idea how many emails you have received, and you don't care. You will have to answer to the manufacturer on that. You have no idea how many people hit your page. You don't care if your page is cell-phone friendly. You don't care if your websites load fast. You don't care if you have professional pictures and videos on your site. You don't care what your closing percentage is and how many appointments you set. If you operate in this old-fashioned way, you are a dinosaur. Hopefully, you will sell your dealership before everybody passes you, and your dealership has lost all its value.

If you are overly dependent on technology, you don't have anybody who is assigned to monitor your virtual showroom, which is everybody who hit your website, your social media, and the incoming emails and phone calls. If you just depend on technology to get you there, you are going nowhere fast. There has to be a balance of salesmanship and technology.

If you lean more one way than the other or ignore one way or the other, you will be lost. It's paramount that you learn and marry the two. As you do, you set yourself up to be on the cutting edge and ahead of the competition. Then your sales and gross will rise.

The key to staying ahead of the game and competition is learning the modern technology and learning how to use it to your advantage and mixing it with time-tested, age-old selling techniques that work.

Why would you not want to grow and change and be on the forefront when it's your money and your business we are talking about? If you want to find more opportunities at your car lot, get back to the basics.

## What Dealers Must Do to Survive

If you are going to keep up with the rapidly changing world of e-media, e-advertising, and e-presence, you will have to hire experts in the field of e-commerce.

You have to dive into the web and learn as much about it as you used to know about newspaper advertising to understand how and why you are spending your money. You also have to do that to have a clue about who you are reaching and how you are reaching them, and to know the ROI on the money you spend reaching them.

Beyond pricing strategies and web displays, you are going to have to learn the language and the methods this new world provides us in the form of reaching your customer database, gathering information from them, informing them of your sales or specials, and even selling them products in the virtual world.

To survive as a dealer, you have three options:

1. Sell your dealership right now

2. Learn it all yourself

3. Get in the game and have managers who manage the modern technology and combine it with the sales processes and techniques that work.

## What Dealers Must Do to Thrive

As a dealer or CEO, it is paramount that you keep up with the ever-changing status and latest developments in search engine optimization (SEO). It may be cumbersome, but it's worth the time, effort, and energy to do so because remaining relevant in this digital age is what separates the winners from the losers. The exciting part is that this dependence on web relevance is going to continue to grow in rapid fashion.

We all have a choice. We can get on board and enjoy the ride, or we can get left behind as we refuse to accept the new world of auto sales and cling to a dying old world. Then we will blame our lack of success in the modern times on change itself, rather than ourselves for not changing, all the while complaining about change and over-emphasizing how wonderful it used to be in the good old days when we just had TV, radio, and print.

**Embracing SEO.** Ignoring the changing world of SEO, and not employing an e-commerce strategy will lead you to poor traffic counts, and it could lead to both poor rankings and penalties you want to avoid. The winners in the world of online brands have long practiced the art of SEO but the losers simply have ignored it as if it was a fad that would go away. It's evolving, but it is not going away, so understanding SEO and having a strategy is increasingly important.

**Implementing speedy mobile traffic optimization.** If you don't implement speedy mobile traffic optimization (MTO), you will lower your very important rankings.

The name of the game is speedy page loading. Having support content that is not supported by the mobile content or that takes too long to load means that your customers have to fight through slow loading and non-supported content to get to your meat and potatoes, and that will kill you.

Typically, responsive sites load slowly enough as it is, and you may want your guests to sign in, register, or fill out an application, so you should avoid non-supportive materials, pop-ups, and overlays that slow you even more.

**Constant monitoring.** Who knew a few years ago that we would be talking about negative SEO and Google penalties? How do you avoid a tanking in your rankings? How do you monitor your SEO, and how can you recover? The only method is constant monitoring and learning SEO and Google management. Failing to monitor can be more catastrophic than not monitoring your sales process, floor plan, or contracts in transit.

**Tracking actions.** The keyword ranking system is not the selling point it once was, as a growing technology field now allows us to track users and their behaviors over a longer time. What method did your customers use to find your site? When they arrived at your site, how long did they stay, and what did they view while they were there? Did they proceed to complete an action that gathered information for you, or did they complete a revenue-producing transaction? If so, how long did it take them to do that, and which route did they travel? Tools such as Kissmetrics have allowed us to track their actions on a whole new level.

To be first on Google, you need to learn Hummingbird algorithms and link building and pursue keywords that are mid-long, long tail, and broad. Doesn't this sound fun? You also need to learn about crosslinking, detailed FAQs, implied and expressed links, and content marketing combined with technical SEO marketing. We have a lot to learn, but we have always been a resilient bunch.

Many latest and greatest new things were going to kill us over the years. We do know for certain that the dealers who learn this game the quickest and apply their learning to the marketplace are going to have a decided advantage over the rest of the dealers. And are we not always searching for an advantage to beat the other guy? It's the competitive fire that got us in this game to begin with and has kept us here all these years.

The ironic thing about the information and technology age is quite simply this: not learning it will surely kill us, but *learning this modern technology aligns us with the greatest ally we have ever known*!

Here is a list of questions dealers and managers need to ask:

1. How user-friendly is your website?

2. Are the general manager and sales managers actively involved in managing the store's web presence?

3. Do any of your managers know how to manage your web presence effectively?

4. What is the turnaround time from when the vehicle arrives through transport or trade-in to when pictures of the vehicle are loaded to the website?

5. Are you still using generic photos? (Please say no.) Do you offer 360 views, videos, or zoom-ins?

6. Do your associates conduct video conversations with your customers via your websites and their mobile devices?

7. If so, is there any system of monitoring these conversations?

8. How do you track and maximize your ROI via Internet advertising?

9. Are you monitoring the e-commerce traffic count via your websites, social media, and the manufacturer's site?

10. Are you managing the hits, leads, and appointments set, shows, and sold?

11. Do you have a special strategy for callers or web hits that are out of your area?

12. Are you committed to a pricing strategy that works?

13. Do you have specialized Internet department representatives?

14. Are the sales associates involved in the lead response process at all?

15. Do you measure and monitor all incoming calls?

16. Who reviews the calls for quality control?

17. Are all of your calls entered in the CRM immediately via manual entry or automated entry?

18. Who is assigned to take the phone, email, or video turnovers?

19. Are all of your manufacturer and dealership sales events placed on all your sites including social media?

20. Who manages your social media/reputation sites?

21. Does your parts and service department have a sufficient presence online?

22. Can customers order parts or set service appointments online?

23. Are all your employee photos professional and up to date?

24. Does your dealership give a good vibe in the photos that are shown?

25. Where do you rank in regards to response time compared to other dealers?

26. Are you still using automated responses?

27. Are you wholesaling parts online?

28. Are you familiar with the terms OEM and SEO?

29. Do you perform email training?

30. How is the communication between the Internet department, the BDC, and the sales department?

31. Are your sites mobile device compatible and made for easy mobile navigation?

32. How quickly does your site download?

33. Do you know what an organic lead is?

34. Are you familiar with the term integrated?

35. Do you ensure that your representatives use proper punctuation and grammar?

36. Do you know what crowdsourcing is?

37. Do you know how you can get negative reviews removed?

38. Which review sites should you pay attention to and why?

39. How can you create raving fans while spending less money?

40. Do you assign leads to managers and sales people?

41. How long are customers on your page?

42. Are you capturing the information of people who visit your page?

43. What are your conversion rates?

44. Are the e-vital statistics discussed in your morning meeting?

45. Are we having fun yet?

# CHAPTER 4

# Gross: Back to the Basics

These days, a lot of people ask, "Where is the gross?" Have we forgotten the processes to hold gross? Most dealerships are processed to death. However, any process without passion isn't any process at all.

Here is a simple example that illustrates the importance of gross: if you only added $300 per car to a dealership that sells 100 units per month, it adds up to an additional $360,000 a year. That is how important gross is.

Gross, just like anything beautiful, will leave you if you don't care for it. One thing is certain: if you don't believe in gross, you will never see it. If you don't believe it is possible, then it is not possible for you. But if you don't believe that you can make gross with all the technology that is available today, then you are crazy.

Dealers are famous for saying: "In our unique market, there are a lot of dealers, and it's cutthroat, so we can't make any money." That is a loser's limp. It's also a lie designed to make you quit without stepping into the ring.

You can make money in any market, but it's going to take some work, and you will have to get acclimated to marrying the modern technology with the old-fashioned techniques that have worked perfectly and always will. That is a positive attitude, and that is having sales skills. If you have a positive attitude and a passionate process, and you inspect what you expect, then you are going to win.

There are dealers in every market in America who practice basic gross techniques, and they outperform the dealers who don't. The dealers who practice basic gross techniques hold daily training meetings, and they get their management involved. They hold gross in the same market as the dealers who say: "Oh, in our unique market, you just can't hold gross."

## The Three Primary Gross Killers

The main excuses for lack of gross are the information age and tough competition. But we know that these are not the biggest gross killers. The biggest gross killers are your salespeople and your managers, and they are suffering from the following three things.

**A bad attitude.** First, they suffer from the bad attitude of falsely believing that good grosses are not attainable in their market. In every market I have been to, they have said the dealership down the street sells cars for triple net losses. It was that way already before the Internet was invented.

The Internet and the competition are no excuses not to work your customers and deals properly. You can't blame these things for your inability to hold gross. You don't believe you can, and you don't try. That is losing before the game begins.

**Lack of structure.** Not having structures or negotiating processes is a sure way to have low grosses. This permeates dealerships, and it's unbelievable to me.

If you sell in a different way to every customer, your sales managers let it happen however it happens, and your salespeople are not trained every day on a structured negotiation process, you are going to have low grosses.

He who fails to plan plans to fail. If you don't have a plan for holding gross, how are you going to hold gross? You can't expect to hold gross if you don't have a negotiation technique.

Also, if you don't practice overcoming the most common objections and the proper verbiage to use in emails to get people in – you don't practice what you are supposed to do to hold gross – then you are not going to hold gross.

**Obliviousness.** The third biggest gross killer is being oblivious to proper pricing strategies on the Internet, supply and demand, and setting appointments without spilling all your beans.

You can't sell fresh trades, rare packages, or hot models cheaply. A book, invoice, or MSRP may not tell the whole story about a car. You may have the only one for 400 miles. If so, you need to get a premium price for it. Conversely, if there are many of them, then sell them for less.

If you have a base model car with every applicable rebate, and you advertise that car, that doesn't mean that you have to sell every car on your lot that has different equipment for a triple net. If you have an aggressive price leader, then have that, but be smart about it and understand that a price leader is a price leader. You don't have to price the rest of your cars that may be more desirable the same way.

There is a certain amount of profit that you need to make. You can't simply hope that customers will come in and that your pricing strategies online are good and that you are going to hold gross. If you pay attention to your core pricing strategies, inspect what you expect on all of your leads, and get manager involvement, it's amazing how your grosses will increase.

The skill of maximizing profits on deals is becoming a lost art. It's replaced by excuses and incompetence. As I go from dealership to dealership, and I speak with the managers, I am appalled at their lack of negotiation skills. The customers come in and say: "I don't want to negotiate. I just want an in-and-out price." Then the sales managers give them their bottom dollar. Far too many sales managers are unfamiliar with basic gross selling techniques. If you are a giveaway artist, a low grosser, and you teach your sales associates to be as incompetent as you are, there is not going to be any gross.

Training in the art of negotiation is shockingly absent in most dealerships today. At the same time, most customers do research online, and they rehearse what they are going to do, so most customers have become much better negotiators than the average sales associate. The customers are getting more for their trade-ins, and they get the new cars cheaply because the salespeople have no techniques. The salespeople don't believe they can hold gross. They believe they have to sell cars cheaply because of the competition or the manufacturer, and therefore, they do.

## The Three Biggest Gross-Killing Closes

The following are the three biggest gross-killing closes that I see repeatedly and fearfully pitched by low-gross artists who are supposed to be automobile retailers but in reality just have a job at a car lot.

The first one goes like this: "Mr. and Mrs. Customer, I will keep lowering the price, and I will keep offering you more for your trade-in until you say yes."

The second one goes like this: "Mr. and Mrs. Customer, I will give you half the holdback, and I will put too much money in your trade-in if you will just take my deal."

The third one, which is awful, is: "Mr. and Mrs. Customer, I will give you the holdback. I will over-promise on the interest rate. I will cheaply sell you a warranty if I need to. I will throw in a paint and fabric protector. I will get it from another dealer and not even charge you the cost that I'm going to incur to get it."

They just give and beg rather than explain the benefit, build the value, and ask the customers questions that are designed to help them pick a vehicle that they want. People are typically willing to pay for something they want.

At the car dealerships I go to, I see many salespeople and managers who beg. They do that because they are not paying attention. They haven't followed the steps to the sale (more on these in Chapter 6). They haven't done fact-finding and investigating. They haven't asked the customers a lot of questions. They haven't done a quality demonstration and presentation. They haven't even walked around the trade to assess the value of it.

Then, when they close a deal, they will high-five and fist-bump and brag as if they have sold a car. But they didn't sell a car; they gave it away.

I have witnessed the lack of negotiation techniques firsthand. I don't know if I sympathize more with the sales associate, the customer who they are putting through this lack of sales technique, or the dealer who isn't making any money.

Clueless sales managers will get involved and make the deal even worse than the untrained sales associates. They will often go straight to the third bad close: "I'll give you all the holdback and give you our best buy rate."

Is it any wonder that the customers complain about a lack of professionalism or positive feelings in the negotiation process? Is it any wonder that most customers hate this? The lack of professionalism, systems, and training is sad.

The best line of cars, the best manufacturer, the best location, the best advertising strategy, or the nicest building is not going to save you if we have a tough economy like we had in '07 and '08.

Having the best people performing processes with passion is what is going to get you there. Trained people who are passionate are going to beat people who aren't passionate. Getting back to the basics is always the answer to every question regarding missed sales gross. Every time you wonder how to increase your grosses, the answer is always to get back to the basics.

## Five Powerful Techniques to Capture Lost Gross

**Start from the top when negotiating.** You can always go down, but you can never go back up in negotiations. Asking full MSRP or addendum on a car is the only acceptable way to start the deal. Not doing so makes a mockery of the MSRP price, and it costs you credibility.

Full MSRP on a car is typically 3.5% to 5% markup to the dealer. If you compare it to other retailers, 5% is laughable. I was reading a magazine the other day where they referred to MarketWatch.com. MarketWatch.com had said that Wal-Mart had an average of 32% markup, and Target had a 46% markup. I don't know if that's accurate but it seems feasible. Also, if you pay your first six months of insurance and don't file a claim, you pay your insurance company a lot more profit than you pay your car dealer even if you paid full sticker. Car dealers have just been very easy to pick on.

Customers will swear that they don't want to negotiate, but if you give them your best price, the first thing they do is write it down and go to another store to negotiate. That small markup of 5% is 5% people want to feel good about.

Even in today's information age, between 10 and 20% of customers will pay MSRP if you have followed the steps, asked them questions so that you know exactly what they want, and done a proper job of showing them that car. If you have valued their time, treated them fairly and professionally, and answered their questions with honesty, and if you are well dressed and well groomed, and you earn the right to ask them to pay full MSRP, about 20% of your customers will do that just because you asked. But you have to ask.

Nobody will volunteer to pay MSRP, but about one out of five customers will pay MSRP if you do a good job and then ask – especially if you have a unit that is in demand, for example, a rare color or a rare package. But don't hold it over the customers' heads and threaten them by saying: "You will have to pay full MSRP, or you won't get this one." And don't try to trick them and manipulate them. Just tell them the truth. Certain cars are worth MSRP. Cheaper is not always better, and better is not always cheaper.

If you do not present the cars well, do not know the answers to the questions the customers have about the cars, do not do a good job of fact-finding and investigating, and do not respect the customers' time, then you have not earned the right to ask for the small percentage of markup. But if you have earned the right, then you deserve a fair profit.

**Teach and coach basic negotiation skills.** As I said earlier, basic negotiation skills are a lost art at dealerships today. Dealers and managers keep saying: "I don't have time to train my people." If you don't have time to train your people, then you must be selling a lot of cars and making a boatload of money. If you train and teach your people how to be more successful and give them an identity, something they can hold on to, they will typically be loyal to you.

It's important to get the customers to commit. If I do this, will you do this? "Mr. Customer, would you allow me to show you a proposal? I understand you said you want to think about it, but allow me to share this with you. If you want to think about it, let me give you all the ingredients to think about. I want to appraise the trade-in, and I want to figure in the payoff. I want to tell you everything, and if I can't excite you enough to make you a deal, that is my fault, not your fault. Would that be fair enough for you?"

Learn these techniques to take customers as far as you can without stopping the deal. We don't stop a deal. We push deals as far as we can. It's amazing what happens when you learn these techniques. Nothing is going to take the place of having the fundamental belief that if you earn the right, you can ask for the money. That is teaching the very basic negotiating skills.

**Have a practiced, drilled, and rehearsed format for negotiating.** If you don't have a practiced, drilled, and rehearsed format for negotiating, then what do you have? I will tell you what you have; you have chaos, low grosses, and confusion. Your customers are unhappy, and so are your managers and salespeople. Everybody is lost. When you are lost, there is no such thing as shortcuts.

Having a format dedicated to the negotiating process is critical. You cannot arrive at your destination without a plan. My personal belief is that providing the customers with a simpler, kinder, version of the "Foursquare" is the best way to do it. I call it a transparent pencil for lack of any other term, the name four square scares people. It has a stigma to it. Many think it is bad, but it's the most customer-friendly and sales-friendly way of doing it because you give the customers all the information upfront, and nothing is hidden. The transparent pencil contains the following:

- The price – the MSRP, the discounted price, or rebate
- The value of the trade-in
- The down payment if there is any
- The payments

Rather than handwriting the transparent pencil, you can print it directly from your CRM tool. It looks a lot like the old foursquare, only there are no lines separating the figures.

Negotiating with the transparent pencil raises the closing percentage, the front-end gross, and the back-end gross. It is the most productive negotiating strategy invented since the four square. If you do not need the additional gross or closing percentage, avoid using it!

The transparent pencil provides the customers with the good feeling of winning. If your customers don't feel good, it doesn't matter if the deal is great. If the dealership is losing $1,000, and the customers don't feel good about it, it's not a good deal. If the dealership is making $3,000, but the customers feel good about it, it's a good deal.

Even if you don't use the transparent pencil, you need to practice, drill, and rehearse some method on a daily basis. Practice the objections you hear every day. Any practiced method gives your sales associate confidence. Confidence turns into gross. Fear turns into a loss of gross.

I know that everyone hates to practice, but dealerships that practice a predetermined method and negotiate a deal the same way every time always hold more gross than dealerships that don't.

**Ask for and work for a down payment on every deal.** No deal ever starts off without asking for a down payment. You should ask for a down payment on every deal, and you should offer the customers lease options and different financial options instead of going straight to a long term of 72 months, or 84 months, and guessing the lowest interest rate possible. Cash is king, and it is the common denominator in most high-grossing deals.

When your initial offer is zero dollars down, then how could you possibly negotiate with the down payment? So practice negotiating the down payment.

It would go like this: "Mr. and Mrs. Customer, if I could show you the advantages and savings of putting down an initial investment on this vehicle, would X amount of dollars be available?" If they say "no," they don't have the money. If they say "yes," then you explain it to them.

All the money they put down on a vehicle as an initial investment is at 0% interest, but if they finance, it's going to have an interest rate on it. Putting down money also puts them in an equitable situation faster. Nothing is better than being in an equitable situation as fast as possible. If, God forbid, they wreck their car, or somebody steals it, etc., their insurance company will pay them the book value of the car. If they are in an inequitable situation, which in the car business is commonly referred to as "upside down," they will be stuck with the overage. So some initial investment always helps them in that regard. Also, when they put down an initial investment, the computer scoring system of most lenders will register that. In addition, the more money they put down, the less they will owe on their car, so the lower their payments will be.

If all those benefits don't convince the customers, then they won't put down any money, but at least you have let them know how advantageous it is.

**Internet pricing strategies.** A lot of sites say: "Call and ask for a price," which you can get away with as long as you have some nice ad leaders. However, many dealers don't understand what to do regarding search engine optimization and how to ensure that they hold gross on the Internet.

How can we hold gross if we have poor web pricing strategies? How can we hold gross if people can't get our prices online? How can we hold gross if we do not use a price leader? How can we hold gross if we do not monitor our Internet presence and update it several times a day every day?

As we have more traffic on our website than in our dealership, we need to have price leaders, which are designed to drive in traffic. However, pricing every unit in our lot at no profit is a gross killer. Leads are generated without spilling all your opportunities for gross on the web. You do need some price leaders, but you also need to be smart and look at some of the pricing strategies of the clever dealers. There are some smart strategies that will let you make a fair profit, but you must do some research and work, and you must implement them.

Making a fair amount of profit starts with the belief that you have earned it. If you are beaten down mentally, and you think that you can't do it and that your Internet strategy will not work, then it won't. Soon enough when we are cradle to grave with one "sales manager", this will simplify in terms of gross holding. In the meantime we had better be ready to make more gross with the current format.

CHAPTER 5

# Coaching – the People Process

Now it's time to look at coaching or what I call the people process. I call it the people process because as you grow your people and add value to them, you grow and add value to your dealership.

The people process is the single most ignored process and the single highest ROI (return on investment) process that any dealer could ever wish to encounter. What you get back for the time, effort, and money you put in here is incredible.

## Why Do Coaching?

Coaching is defined as a training or improvement process.[9] Dealerships are very process-driven, and the manufacturers have been hammering the retailers for processes since long before I started in the industry. A passionless process is as useful as a back pocket on a shirt.

Many think that they will be successful just by having lots of processes without teaching and growing salespeople, but that's not true. Several years ago, one manufacturer bought all the dealerships in the largest metro areas of a particular state. They were convinced they knew how to sell cars better than the dealers and that the dealers were bad. They thought they were going to teach the dealers a lesson. Sure enough, it didn't work out for them, and they couldn't figure out why since they had some great processes. They had gone to one price, they appraised cars up front, and they wouldn't hire any experienced "car people." They were able to turn and run without admitting failure because the dealers were

---

[9]    Coaching [Def. 1]. (n.d.). *Oxford Dictionaries Online*. Retrieved December 18, 2015, from http://www.oxforddictionaries.com/definition/learner/coaching

suing them, but they knew there would be litigation beforehand. They got out because their results were underwhelming at best since they didn't have an understanding of retail sales.

Great processes with uneducated or uninspired people are the roads to nowhere. If you have average processes but great and inspired people, you will find a way to win. Inspiring your people is paramount. It's the key, much more important than your processes.

The dealerships that bring extraordinary results to the table, the dealerships that are above and beyond, the ones that overachieve, are your Cal Worthingtons in California and your Lynn Hickey Dodges in Oklahoma City. They are the ones with the best people.

Since cars began to be mass-produced in the United States in 1903, the dealerships that have done an extraordinary job all have one thing in common. It's not a certain manufacturer, location, or advertising gimmick. They were all adamant about sales training. Go figure.

If you are excellent at building a team of sales professionals, growing them as sales professionals, adding value to them, and making them believe in something, then that teamwork will make the dream work. You make them understand their part of being on the team. You make them understand all the intricacies of selling cars and dealing with people. You teach them how to handle any objections that the customers may have and how to make the customers feel good about their decision.

As a coach, you teach people to be better at what they are doing. When you know better, you do better. It's a training and development process for improvement. The reason you do it every day, and in my opinion twice a day, is because you are searching for perpetual improvement. Forecast it, track it, discuss it, and improve it.

It's a fact that the people who are the best at what they do have the greatest chance to win. If you were comparing the car business to the NFL or NBA, it is the team that has the best players that wins a very high percentage of their games, not the team that has the newest field or gym. The teams that recruit and train the best talent are the ones winning. It's the same thing in auto sales; the best players win. To make your players better, you have to coach them.

## The Common Approach

You won't be able to hire top-notch salespeople and top-notch managers with a good attitude from other dealerships on a consistent basis. Salespeople and managers who come from other dealerships are often malcontent where they are at, or they have personal issues. It's very rare that they are stars that other dealers didn't pay or were made to work too many hours, as they like to claim. The odds are stacked against building a winning team with this method.

People typically leave their job because they are unsuccessful or unhappy there. Often due to a lack of leadership. If you think you can build your future by hiring top-notch salespeople and managers who have worked for but not been trained by other dealerships, you are wrong. It's not going to work. They weren't trained there and you are getting them untrained! I'm not saying they can't be trained, but they don't come ready made.

The old theory is: "That is the way I have always done it, and I don't want to invest in these guys because they are going to leave anyway." If that is your attitude, you probably should go ahead and advertise your dealership in *Automotive News* while it still has value, so you don't take a huge loss as progressive dealers pass you. The dealers who do coach, improve, and add value to their people are the ones that are going to win.

Virtually every dealership in America routinely promotes top sales associates into management. We promote our top sales associates because these associates have demonstrated the ability to sell cars at a high level. However, selling cars at a high level as an individual is a totally different skill set than coaching a team to perform at a high level, adding value to it, and growing it. The two skills are actually quite the opposite of one another. One is an individual thing, and the other is an understanding of the big picture.

When we make these promotions, we fail the newly promoted people because we don't develop them. We typically give them little if any coaching or leadership training, and due to their lack of preparedness, they are almost certainly going to fail. They haven't done anything to understand the big picture to be coaches. They have just sold a lot of cars as individuals, so that is what they are concentrating on.

When we combine the dealerships' lack of commitment to developing the newly promoted people and these people's lack of commitment to learning what coaches and leaders do, it results in failure nearly every time.

Rather than investing in developing our people, we simply hope – we get on the hope program. Then after the promotions happen, we remain in the hope program, and we hope that the other managers will show them the ropes of being sales managers.

Of course, the other managers never received any leadership training or coaching training either. That is why some of them had to be fired. But we still hope they will train the new promotions how to be managers. Since they are mediocre or average at best, it's a long shot to hope that they will somehow make them into leaders and coaches.

We hope they will teach them about deal structure, appraising cars, submitting deals, and ordering cars. We hope that they will train them on the people process and management functions that managers have. We hope these new promotions are what will grow our business, despite the fact that we haven't done anything to assist them or tee them up for success.

Then we hope that our new promotions don't get immersed in e-mails, frazzled by phone calls, dazed by data, and pulverized by pressure, or even worse, they get entitled by their new title. If they become entitled by their title, they will be hard on the sales staff. They will take on the top guns and let everybody know they are the bosses. They will be more interested in being the bosses than selling cars and growing the business. The result will be poor sales and excuses.

We hope that the lack of leadership skills won't breed stress and a poor attitude and excuses and blaming and ineffectiveness. But history has taught us that an onslaught of these plagues will soon stymie our new managers, and soon they will resemble someone who has taken a drink from a fire hydrant; blown away by the challenges and lack of training. It's a little bit their fault, but it's mostly our fault.

The excuse for such a flawed business practice is: "That's how we have always done it." This begs the question: How could such a production-oriented business repeatedly practice such a flawed method that continually results in a high rate of failure? No one gets replaced more than sales managers and salespeople. Thinking: "That's the way we have always done it" is old-school thinking that will run you out of business.

## A Wise Investment

Is this 1980 or 1990? Obviously, it is not. And do we continue doing everything just like we did then? Lacking the vision to invest in growing our people is much more expensive than investing and growing them. Lacking this vision is what is causing the turnover, the lack of sales, and the poor CSI (Customer Service Index, a survey where the customers say how happy they are with the dealership and the experience they had).

The lack of investment that I'm talking about is not necessarily monetary. Aren't our time and energy investments as well? Continually starting over with new people has a high cost and so does the customer service we are not giving our customers as we keep replacing managers. Think of how our sales and profits suffer and the litigation that could happen from having managers who don't know what they are doing. Think about the low gross, low net, and low employee satisfaction.

When we fail to train our managers to be coaches and build something, everything suffers. If we are successful but didn't build something ourselves, then we are riding a wave that we didn't create, and we don't know how long that is going to last. The wave is going to end, and then we are going to be looking for another wave.

Don't you agree that confident, inspired, and well-trained associates produce much better results than beat-down, stressed out, and overwhelmed associates? It is a common sense question.

Will Rogers is one of my favorite guys. He stated: "the problem with common sense is that it isn't so common."[10] When I see dealers repeat the mistake of not coaching their people, it occurs to me that common sense is a flower that doesn't grow in everyone's garden.

Dealers fall for the excuses some of their managers are great at giving. The managers' say: "There aren't any good people out here to hire any more," or "Why develop them when they are going to leave anyway?" This is a loser's mantra to be avoided. *People who are good at making excuses are seldom good for anything else.* The good people won't leave, as long as you are fair with them. If you are the one who showed them the way, that carries a lot of weight.

Start developing and coaching your people. Start today because other people are catching on to it and beginning to do it. If you don't do it, you are going to get left in their rear-view mirror. As you fall further and further behind, they are stepping on the gas, and you don't have a gas pedal to step on because you are still hiring people who haven't been taught anything about coaching or leadership.

Allow me to share some examples of great players not performing well as coaches or team builders. Magic Johnson seemed to have all the ingredients and charisma in the world.

---

10    *Will Rogers says...* (n.d.). Retrieved December 14, 2015, from
      http://www.willrogers.com/quotes.html

He was a high school champion, an NCAA champion, a five-time NBA champion, a gold medalist, MVP of the league, and MVP of the finals. But when he took over as coach of the Lakers, he won only 31% of his games. Magic wasn't a very good coach, in spite of being a great player and all the other things that he had going for him.

Michael Jordan, a six-time champion, and MVP all six times, is perhaps the greatest basketball player of all time. But he struggled even to make the playoffs as an executive with Washington and Charlotte when he bought into the NBA. Building a team and dominating as an individual are two different skills.

Bart Starr won five championships and two Super Bowls as a quarterback for Green Bay, but he had a coaching record of 52 wins and 76 losses. He was once quoted saying: "Coaching was the greatest mistake I ever made."[11] The examples are many.

This is how badly you need coaching: Peyton Manning is the all-time leading touchdown passer in NFL history, and he will go down as one of the best quarterbacks in NFL history. His dad was an NFL quarterback, and his brother Eli Manning is a quarterback for the Giants. So Peyton has grown up in the NFL. Nevertheless, he has a quarterback coach. He gets coaching because he needs it to stay sharp and improve.

Tiger Woods, who was the greatest golfer on Earth at one time and had the best swing on Earth, employed a swing coach. He did that because he wanted to win. He will go down as one of the top tour winners of all time.

Coach and train your team every day. Zig Ziglar said: "People often say that motivation doesn't last. Well, neither does bathing –

---

[11]   Kirchen, R. (2013, May 15). Packers legend Bart Starr: Coaching was 'greatest mistake I made' - *Milwaukee - Milwaukee Business Journal*. Retrieved December 14, 2015, from http://www.bizjournals.com/milwaukee/blog/2013/05/packers-legend-bart-starr-coaching.html

that's why we recommend it daily."[12] If you want to get on top and stay on top, you will have to do this. Whether you are prepared for it or not, the future is going to be here.

If you have been in the car sales business for more than just a little while, then you know that the good economic times that we are experiencing right now are a period when bad habits are formed. Good times make bad habits. During these times when the economy is good, sales are plentiful, and we set records, so we pat ourselves on the back.

However, when times tighten up, just like they did in '07, and '08, many dealers seem very surprised and unprepared. During tougher economic times, we must depend on our people to be better than the competition's people. Survival won't come down to our brand or our location or our advertising dollars. Our people being better than the competition's people is what it's going to come down to, and there is only one way to make our people better.

This is when some businesses are forced to sell to their competitors, and some are forced to close their doors. Why wait until the wolf is at the door? Why not have the best team even in good economic times, rather than waiting until the bad economic times to start training? Training picks up at every dealership in bad economic times.

The following is my five-point strategy for equipping dealerships for the future.

## Five-Point Strategy

**Make a plan to identify, hire, and promote coaches.** Great coaches are not always the top producers. They are easily recognizable because of their communication. They are team players, and they encourage others to do the best they can do.

---

[12]  *People often say that motivation doesn't last.* (n.d.). Retrieved December 14, 2015, from http://www.ziglar.com/quotes/zig-ziglar/people-often-say-motivation-doesnt-last

Many sales managers believe that their job is to appraise cars, submit deals, handle mad customers on the phone, and open and close the store. But that is the least of what they need to be great at. Employing the old-fashioned, visionless managers whose primary skills are taking credit for others' success, blaming others for failures, and sitting on their butts wondering where all the good salespeople are, will kill you in today's market. Those sales managers have outrun their resumes. Their resumes are in the rear-view mirror, and their best days are not ahead of them.

If you want to go to the past instead of the future, then keep hiring those managers who don't know how to coach, build a team, and add value to people. Those managers typically have limited coaching skills. They are a dime a dozen; they are everywhere.

If the managers aren't improving your people, then they must go. Our industry is crowded with selfish people who don't have a clue about growing a team. A coach deeply cares for others. It's a sacrifice to coach and grow people. But when people grow, production grows exponentially. This is multiplying versus adding.

Every dealership needs a top official to be their coach. A top official – a dealer, a general manager, or a general sales manager – must be a great coach. If your dealer, general manager, and general sales manager are not great coaches, you are doing it the old-fashioned way. Then you will be beaten by the new generation.

**Implement daily training.** Focus on developing leadership, teamwork, communication, and attitude. If you can help people become confident, that confidence will cover a multitude of sins. Success is 80% attitude. That is what every sales trainer says. Doesn't it make sense to nurture the attitude of your sales staff if it is 80% of what you do? You can do it by investing in and developing your people via online training, seminars, and, most importantly, daily in-house training by your in-house coach.

If you don't have an in-house coach who is a general manager, general sales manager, or dealer, you have to hire a coach to come in and train your people. If you don't do that, then others will pass you. When you train your people, you secure your future.

I like to have training sessions twice a day, but even if you do it once a day, at least you are making an effort. You can have your first session in the morning when the first shift arrives, and when the second shift arrives is a great time for another 20-minute session. Typically, car lots have two shifts. People, especially salespeople, have limited attention spans. For that reason, I limit our training sessions to 20 minutes.

I make these sessions interactive. We might do some role-plays with cell phones where we make phone calls or answers phone calls. We might also do meet-and-greets and objection overcoming. This training is planned and positive, and it's designed for a specific purpose: to add value by growing your sales associates' skills.

Let me caution you: There should be no negativity, no "how great I was when was a salesperson," and no "how crappy of a job you guys are doing" at these meetings. Those training meetings are not allowed because those are not training meetings. I'm talking about strategically planned and purposeful sessions designed to grow the skill set of your sales team to add value to your people. Coaches need to remember that the training is about the people they are training, not them.

**Implement a team leader/liner-closer system.** I promote a team leader/liner-closer system in every dealership that I turn around or take over because I believe this is the only way to work. For one thing, a team leader/liner-closer system promotes growth. Watching people grow as leaders is a beautiful thing.

If you are not currently doing so, implement a team leader/liner-closer system now. The results are positive as each deal is given more attention.

Monitor the team leaders for indicators of leadership abilities. Some have a God-given gift for inspiring others and getting the best out of them. Look for those people; they are more precious than diamonds.

The extra pay for team leaders is minimal. You only have to give them a small salary. Then you give them 5%, maybe 7.5% of the commission per deal of the 8 to 10 people who are on the team leaders' teams. If your pay plan is 25%, the sales associates get 20%, and the team leaders get 5%. If your pay plan is 30%, you may give 22.5% to the sales associates and 7.5% to the team leaders. That is on each deal, and that is going to teach them skills. The only true cost incurred is a small salary. Even if you don't go to the liner-closer system, structure a sales pay plan that rewards achievers.

On a side note: Pay out your commissions weekly; don't do it just monthly. It's essential that your finance department processes the deals quickly. Salespeople typically live paycheck to paycheck. Bills are paid paycheck to paycheck, meals are bought paycheck to paycheck, and children are supported paycheck to paycheck. So process those deals quickly and pay weekly commission. Let your sales staff know how important it is that you pay them accurately and in a timely manner. If they know it's important to you, and you pay weekly, it is going to help you a lot.

**Eliminate selfish team members.** Regardless of their perceived irreplaceable skill set, eliminate those with a me-first and that's-not-my-job attitude. Me-first people are easily replaced, and the team always rises when the selfish stars are cut.

Avoid excuses such as "I can't replace them because they are the best salespeople, managers, paperhangers (the people who get the deals bought), deal-closers, or desk people I have." If they are selfish, and they are not helping other people, then they are hurting you, and they can't be there. You can't have selfish people on your team. The chain is only as strong as the weakest link.

Saying that you can't replace those people and so on is wrong. If you want a bunch of selfish people, and you think you are going to win with them, go ahead and try. Pretty soon, you are going to get passed by all the people who have understood the importance of growing, mentoring, and adding value to people.

**Commit to the coaching process.** Commit to the coaching process right now and go all in. You have to be prepared to place the people with true coaching skills above all others. Doesn't common sense tell us that the more developed our sales teams' skills are, the more successful we will be? Then why would we not insist on developing them? Why would that not be first on our priority list?

If you have to hire an outside coach to start the process of teaching your potential coaches, by all means get the process started right now. Good coaches will improve and inspire your team exponentially. They will help your team achieve their highest levels of production. They will lift the spirit and confidence of the entire dealership, and they make everyone better. What is that worth?

Better people produce better results. Good desk people and finance people and decent closers are much easier to find than good coaches. Start your coaching search right now. The choice is yours; you can get serious about developing your people, or you can begin looking for a buyer while your dealership still has value.

We teach our salespeople to sell what they see rather than see what they can sell. That means to sell the car that is on the lot rather than have the dealer trade and bring in another car. Sales managers and dealers need to learn the same thing. Work with the salespeople you have rather than wish that you had others or hope that some amazing salespeople who are mad at their current job are going to change their attitude and be good. That is not going to happen.

Stop waiting for great salespeople to dawn your doorstep for a job. Start working with what you have. Take the people who come through your door and improve them. It's about perpetual improvement. Make them better every day by training every day.

I hope these five steps have helped you understand how important coaching is. It is that important to me. It is that important to any of you who have ever done it. All the extraordinary dealers have done that. If you add value to each individual, doesn't that add value to the team?

Great salespeople and great sales managers have to be homegrown, so you have to understand how to grow them. When you grow them, they will be loyal to you. Then you will be the Jerry Maguire in their life: the one who shows them the money.

Invest time in your people by teaching them. If you hire a coach to train them, charge it to your advertising budget. As your people grow, your sales grow, and as your sales grow, the value of your dealership grows.

Investing time in your people is the greatest investment you can make. We all know dealerships that have great locations or product lines that don't sell cars. But there is no such thing as a dealership with great people that struggles.

# CHAPTER 6

# Sales Skills Training: What to Train and Why It Matters

The common denominator for sales teams that win big, do the extraordinary, and set sales records is that they train with the dealerships and salespeople that do exactly that.

If you get training for yourself, you add value to yourself, and if you train your team, you add value to your team.

We have had sales trainers and leadership trainers for many years, and now we have coaching trainers. I can think back to all the people who I learned from. It goes all the way back to reading Zig Ziglar, who was one of my favorites. Zig had many great insights, and he taught us how to sell and how to be motivated.

If you want to stay on the bottom in sales, then do what the guys at the bottom do. They learn just enough to be mediocre. Their thought process is: "I know how to do this already. I have already learned it," and they don't put any time into developing themselves in the business.

When you don't seek to train, you don't add to your skills. Then you end up stuck in a certain process or gear, but you brush it off and say: "Oh, well. It's just a numbers game. Either they will buy or they won't."

The lies that you tell yourself are always the most harmful lies. You may tell yourself that you are doing fine and that it's not your fault that your sales numbers are low. You might blame it on the managers, the weather, the line of cars, or the location. My favorite excuse is: "Here in our community, the competition is very tough. My competition advertises the cars so cheaply that I can't sell a lot of cars here. I'm not successful because I'm victim of a difficult place."

When you stop externalizing the reasons for your failure, you decide that you are going improve and train. If you are a dealer or a general manager, you decide to train your people. Then all of a sudden, you start improving.

The steps to the sale are an important part of what you should train. Every dealership has these steps in some form. I have a seven-step process, and if you follow it, you will sell more cars. I will now lay out these steps to you.

## Step 1: The Meet-and-Greet

The first step in the sale is the meet-and-greet. But before the meet-and-greet, you should make sure you are properly dressed and groomed. People will judge you based on your appearance. We can act like people don't judge each other, but they do. You need a certain confidence, and that will come through a groomed appearance as well as sales training.

As you meet and greet the customers, you shake everybody's hands. You don't ignore the spouses or the kids. I always shake hands with the first person I come up to, whether it is the man or the woman. I always say hi to the kids or ask them if they are there to help mom and dad, or whomever they accompany, buy a car.

Shaking people's hands and introducing yourself to them sounds like something that would be easy. However, you would be surprised and perhaps even terrified if you watched what many salespeople do during their introduction to the customers. They haven't practiced it. Typically, they say something like: "Can I help you? Is somebody helping you?"

During the meet-and-greet, it is important to make eye contact and have a good posture, what some call confidence posture or power posture.

# Step 2: Fact-Finding and Investigating

Right after the meet-and-greet, it is time for fact-finding and investigating. This is where the rubber meets the road. You can't be a good salesperson if you are not good at fact-finding and investigating. It's going to separate you from the rest. You can't spout off information to someone without knowing all the details. If you do, you are guilty of malpractice. Then you mess up more deals than you make.

There are many questions you must ask the customers, and you must get them involved. You have to become a professional question asker. When you are good at asking questions, you know how to ask one question that leads to another question.

You also need to learn to listen between the lines. Customers will say a lot without saying it in plain English. Sometimes it's what they don't say. They talk around it. Their body language can also tell you a lot. Typically, when you meet customers, they don't like, trust, or respect you yet because they haven't had time to get to know you.

As soon as you meet and greet your customers, you evaluate their posture. You evaluate their eye contact. I have had customers with all kinds of body language. Some would try to turn away from me during the meet-and-greet, and every salesperson has experienced those customers. Others have been very friendly and gregarious and acting like they were happy to see me. I have also had customers who were very standoffish. This is where you gauge their body language and try to understand what is going on with them.

I don't know how you can be in sales and not realize the power of understanding body language. For example, if the customers have their arms crossed and folded, you can't sell them anything yet because they are not open to listening. You don't talk business with somebody who has a closed body language. You don't talk business with a lady who is clutching her purse like you are about to steal it from her. You don't talk business and try to close someone who is trying to stand up or get away from you.

Every deal has to open before it can close. You can't close deals with customers who are not listening to you, so you need to learn how to read their body language. You have body language as well, and you have to control it. You open the deal by talking about family, occupation, recreation, and them – the customers. Anybody opens up when talking about those four things.

As you get into your fact-finding and investigating, there is a lot you need to find out to help your customers. If the customers say, "We're looking for a $7,000 car," you can't just start looking for a $7,000 car. You don't know that they have equated the $7,000 to be what they think their trade (previous car) is worth. You don't know that they have equated that to a $200 or $300 payment. You don't know what they are actually looking for in a car. Unless you ask questions, you won't be able to find them a car. Real salespeople do their selling in their listening.

Typically, most dealerships spend between $20,000 and $100,000 a month on marketing, and they usually have sales going on. When customers come to your dealership, you ask, "Did you hear about our sale?" Then you explain the sale to them, and you ask them if they are there to see anyone specific or if they have worked with anyone there before. From there, you ask: "Who is the lucky one? Who is getting a car, truck, or van?" Then you ask: "Will you be adding or replacing your car?" Next you ask: "Is there a payoff balance on your trade in? You keep on asking questions so that you can help the customers properly. The more you ask and listen, the more you will be able to help your customers.

A lot of salespeople just ask, "Can I help you?" When the customers reply that they are just looking, the salespeople ask them what they are looking for. Then, when the customers say: "Oh, we're looking for a $7,000 car," the salespeople run off looking for cars at that price without asking any further questions. The best thing you can do is invest time to listen to the customers and do professional fact-finding and investigating.

You should also assess their needs and wants. Ask them about their trade: "What do you have in your current vehicle that you would like in another vehicle?" "What do you not like about your vehicle that you want in a vehicle?"

Listen so well that your customers can't ignore you. Be a brilliant question asker and listener. Then you will find out a lot about how to help them get a car. The questions that you ask every customer are going to move you forward.

This step is paramount. If you don't do it properly, you won't be able to go to the next step because your needs assessment, fact-finding, and investigating are going to determine what your next step of the sale will be.

## Step 3: Setting the Stage

The third step is setting the stage. This step in my sales process differs from many other people's steps. This is where we have to adapt to the modern times. The steps of the sale are still golden, and you still do all of them, but now there has to be this added third step of setting the stage.

Through your fact-finding and investigating, you might have discovered that your customers have been on the Internet with your business development center. You may have found out that they have been to other dealerships and need specific help with financing or equity challenges. Perhaps they have been here before, and they have picked a car they want. All you have to do is go to your sales manager, get your stock number, and work the deal.

Then you might find out that these customers are "credit-challenged." They have answered an ad that said, "We will finance anybody." You might find out that these customers have a car they have a negative equity of $8,000 on. You may have come across a customer who says: "All I'm interested in is lowering my payment." You may have somebody who has a farm rebate from the government, and he or she wants to buy a farm truck.

Because of the many variables, you can't treat all your customers the same way at this time, and that is why you set the stage. At this point, you go to the sales desk and explain to the sales manager the situation you have on your hands. The manager is the only one who can tell you what you do next, so this manager needs to introduce himself or herself to the customers and set the stage. Often, if you are an excellent and seasoned salesperson, you can set the stage, but you still have to involve the management.

You can set the stage a lot of different ways. Typically, you will begin with filling out a guest sheet. You could also go right to the inventory and get the trade appraised.

## Step 4: Selecting Unit, Doing Demo Drive and Presentation, and Appraising Trade

Regardless of what happens in Step 3, in Step 4, you select a unit, do a demo drive and presentation, and get the customers' trade appraised. I always do a trial close on a demo drive.

It is very important that you do an active trade-in appraisal with the customers at this time. I have been in this business for over two and a half decades, and I can tell you that people sometimes forget that the tires are bald, and they forget about the dings and dents and scratches. They sometimes forget about some of the reason they wanted to trade.

As you walk around their car with them, you never criticize it. Again, what you do is ask questions. For example, ask:
- How did this dent get here?
- What about this scratch?
- When was the last time you bought tires?
- Have you done all the maintenance on the vehicle?
- Do you have the maintenance records?
- How did you get a cracked windshield? (Some people's insurance company will cover that.)

When it's time for the test drive, it's very important that you have done your fact-finding and investigating in Step 2, and that in Step 3 of setting the stage, the sales manager has helped you select vehicles that fit your customers.

When you get back to the car lot from the test drive, you will ask your customers if this is the car they can see themselves owning. The customers will answer your question, and at that time, you have to listen closely because they may tell you something about the car they don't like. If you have picked a car that your customers get excited about, their body language is good, and there is no reason not to do a trial close, then do a trial close.

I believe you push every deal through all the steps no matter what. Only the customers can stop deals. We never stop deals. What I want you to say is: "Allow me to show you a proposal on this car." At this point or another, the customers often say, "We want to think about it" or "We want to shop around." Then you reply: "I understand, but I want to show you all the pieces of the puzzle. If you want to think about it, I want you to have all the pieces so that you can think about the entire puzzle. I want to give you all the ingredients."

I am always positive and tell them that I believe I will offer them a deal that is good enough that they will go ahead and make it since they like the car well enough to want to own it.

The most important thing you say is this: "Mr. and Mrs. Customer, if I can't make you a deal that's good enough for you to accept tonight, that's not your fault; that is my fault. It's my job to make the deal." When I tell the customers that it would be my fault, not their fault if I couldn't find a car or make a deal good enough for them, I let them off the hook.

When the customers agree that it would be your fault, not theirs, you say: "Let me go ahead and do my job and show you the entire process. I want you to see the whole thing front to back.

Come on in. Would you like something cold or warm to drink while I get this proposal ready for you?" Then you bring them in.

This is the best language you can use during a trial close. If you don't want to do it this way, you will miss a lot of opportunities.

## Step 5: Write-Up, Presentation, and Close

The write-up, presentation, and close that take place in Step 5 are very important. You must learn them, practice them, drill them, and rehearse them. It's an everyday thing that you do. You can't do every one of them differently; you have to do them the same way every time. In my opinion, some presentations are better than others, but the one thing I have to impress upon you is that there is no way you can do it differently every time.

Also, there is no way you can be good at the write-up, presentation, and close without practice. These are some of the things that you should work on every single day on your car lot. But don't practice on actual customers.

When you are on Step 5 doing the write-up, presentation of the figures, and the close, you have to understand the basic objections that you will encounter, and you have to be good at overcoming them. The people who do this are called closers. If you go right to Step 5, and you try to close the deal with the customers before you know anything about them, then you are not a closer. Closers know how to open. The purpose of Step 2 – fact-finding and investigating – is to open the deal. After the deal is closed, a common rookie maneuver is to buy the car back. Buying the car back is still convincing the customers what a great deal they got or what they saved. That is all done. The customers may be nibbling at this time, but you do have to shut that down.

## Step 6: Delivering the Vehicle

Then you go into Step 6, which is delivering the vehicle. The delivery of the vehicle is very important. A lot of salespeople like to skip this step, or they do the "Four *C*'s Delivery": See the car, see the keys, see the curb – see you later.

Before the delivery, you have had the vehicle completely cleaned, detailed, and filled up with gas so that it's ready to go. Then, at the delivery, you explain how everything works, and you help the customers move their things from their trade into the new car.

You want to do a professional delivery because your next step is asking for referrals and following up.

## Step 7: Asking for Referrals and Following Up

Step 7 is the final step. As I deliver the car to the customers, I congratulate them. What is a natural response when somebody says "Congratulations"? "Thank you!" They thank me. It's very important that you do this.

Then when you ask for referrals, you put your business cards in the vehicle. You might also have a video where you ask for referrals that you can forward from your phone to the customers' phone.

If the customers say: "Oh, I don't feel comfortable giving away anybody's information" when you ask for referrals, it means you haven't done your job well enough. The customers will give you referrals when you have done a great job as a salesperson.

Many dealerships have referral money that they give customers, and this will make the customers help you more. Some dealerships don't do that, and some salespeople have to pay out of their pocket.

Follow-up is also extremely important. Keep up with your customers. Use the information you enter in the CRM to send them birthday cards, anniversary cards, Christmas cards, and so on.

These steps of the sale are what will separate you from other dealerships. They will keep you on track and help you be consistent in what you do.

# The 7 Steps to the T.O.

Are your managers and sales associates well versed in the art of the turnover?

I dare you to inspect what you expect. If your team flunks the seven steps of the sale and misses out on a proper T.O., you are missing a lot of business. There are no reasons, only excuses. This is completely controllable. Managers must get back in touch with the sales side of sales management. Mastering this nearly extinct skill is both the quickest and surest way to raise your sales numbers.

Most dealerships perform some form of sales associate training. Regardless of how misguided or under supported it is, there is at least an attempt. However, less than 20% of dealerships train their managers. After all, they have a management title, so they couldn't possibly improve their skills. Besides, who could train them? Doesn't their title ensure that they are so proficient at what they do that improvement is not an option?

How often does your dealership practice the sales-to-management handoff known as the T.O. (turnover) in our industry? Isn't prioritizing what is important an ownership or management function? I can assure you that when your dealership implements proper T.O.s, the closing percentage and grosses will go up significantly. Suddenly everyone will agree on the importance of a proper T.O. and say: "Why didn't we focus on this sooner?"

All too frequently, as I go into stores, I see areas where money is left on the table. One of the biggest areas is the lack of performing proper T.O.s.

## Seven Steps for Productive T.O. "Handoffs"

1. **The manager meet-and-greet.** Sales managers must roam the showroom and shake *all* prospects' hands, thanking them for coming out and planting seeds of hope and positivity.

It should be some form of: "Hi, I'm Roger, the sales manager here, thanks for coming out to our ___ sale. What is your name (ask all parties and shake all hands)? I see you are with John. You couldn't have picked a better day or a better salesperson. Thanks again for coming out. I will see you soon."

*Please be advised: This is not a T.O. and is not a long conversation. It's a manager meet-and-greet.

Typically, if the customers ask about skipping steps or are in a hurry – if they ask for an appraisal or any other mode of step-skipping – then the managers can deflect the question and pass it back to the sales associates. "John, be sure and get me a trade appraisal with all the information on it, and I will personally evaluate Nate and Erin's trade. Nate, Erin, since commodities exchanges are more valuable than an outright purchase, low wholesale auction value is always the outright purchase price. But the good news is that I may be able to offer you $500 to $3,000 more for your trade depending on which of our vehicles you select and test-drive. John, please bring me the stock number, and I will personally handle the proposal. Thanks again for giving us an opportunity to exceed your expectations. I will see you in a few minutes." This doesn't take long, and it allows the managers to shake other hands as well as tee up the T.O.

2. **No blame game allowed.** The managers are not allowed to make the sales associates chase them down for a T.O. and grill them for five minutes about "Why do you need a T.O.?" or "Why are they already at the door," etc. Whose fault it is and why the customers made it to the door are of lesser importance than saving the deal. *The top priority is salvaging the deal by getting face to face with the customers immediately.*

The reason a deal is slipping is typically both because of the managers' lack of attention to the deal and the salespeople being afraid or untrained. However, the managers and the sales associates must learn to execute the handoff properly.

The associates must learn to remain seated if the customers stand from the negotiating table, asking the customers to "Please have a seat for me, I have an idea." After the customers sit down, the associates should get a manager.

During the introduction of the managers and the T.O. process, the associates should remain quiet. All the associates must be trained to nod their head appropriately when the managers are asking questions, but they are prohibited from talking or answering questions unless they are asked.

The actual introduction should go something like this: "This is Roger, our manager." That is all the associates say unless the managers specifically address them.

If the customers get up and do not sit back down, the sales managers are forced to introduce themselves without a proper introduction. That introduction is strategic as well. The managers walk straight to the clients and position the meeting to take place between the clients and the door. Upon introducing themselves, the managers are forced to take control quickly and ask the customers to have a seat for a "moment of your time."

If the managers or the associates chase the customers to the door, the likelihood of a successful T.O. decreases dramatically. Regardless of whether the associates introduce the managers or the managers introduce themselves, the associates remain silent from then on.

The managers' attention to the sales floor is tremendously important here. The associates are not allowed to verbalize the reasons the customers are leaving without buying, and they are not allowed to answer any of the questions that the managers ask the customers. The associates must be trained to walk towards the designated seating area simultaneously with the managers while the managers are asking the customers to have a seat.

3. **All T.O.s happen when all progress halts.** The progress could stop at Step 1 at the meet-and-greet, or it could stop at Step 2 or anywhere through Step 7.

   Regardless of where it stops, the managers must get involved right then without fear or hesitation. The managers then assist the customers towards the next step of the sale. This is why the managers must manage the showroom floor and why they must be *focused* and pay attention to each customer.

   I always laugh when dealerships have large flat screen monitors to watch each CRM entry, and then they page or chase down salespeople after the deal turns "red" or the time frame appears out of whack. Really? So exactly what purpose did that large CRM monitor serve? Is it an opportunity to chew the salespeople's butt or fire them? A written sales log with the time the up (customer) was taken would have accomplished the same thing. Paying attention to the lot and the sales floor is and always will be the most effective way to manage each deal.

   Managers must be part guard dog on the lot. Having a manager who is proficient at getting customers into the showroom is a tremendous sales tool, especially on high traffic days when many customers can go unseen. I strongly believe in a managed sales floor. If managers are involved early and often, it is miraculous how much smoother things go and how many more customers are entered into CRM, written up, closed, delivered, and followed up with.

4. **The managers must quickly take control of the situation on the T.O.** After greeting all parties involved with a handshake and a smile, the managers should ask questions to get the customers open before ever attempting to close them. A quick evaluation of body language and a few questions will allow the managers to know exactly what the customers are feeling.

The managers already know the answer to many of these questions, but the idea is to get the customers talking. Opening the sale is the beginning of closing it. Following the customers towards the door is toxic to a car deal, so the customers must be asked to have a seat.

The managers cannot be overbearing, talking too much and listening too little, or rushing the process in an attempt to power-close the customers while standing up and without due process. It's a fatal move, a deal killer.

Immediately after the managers shake the clients' hands, the managers should ask the clients: "Please do me a favor; have a seat right here for me." If the customers object to having a seat, the managers should respond: "I really appreciate your time and your desire to shop around. Please allow me a few moments to show you the entire deal so that you have all the information to think about. I promise I will work quickly. I wouldn't expect you to buy without all the information. C'mon, I insist. (Walking towards the desired seating area) Would you like water, coffee, or soda?"

5. **Questions are the answer.** After sitting the customers down in the showroom, the managers should ask the same fact-finding questions that sales associates ask during Step 2 of the sales process. The managers can go through these quickly to determine which route is best for putting together a deal. The managers must show genuine interest while asking the questions they typically already have the answers to and listen intently while the customers lay out a roadmap of how to sell them a car. Remember: The T.O. happens at different stages of the process, from Step 1 through Step 7.

Here are some sample questions:

- How has Johnny salesman treated you?
- How did you hear about our sale?
- What questions do you have?
- Do you have a trade (previous car)?
- Is the trade financed? If so, what is the payoff or payments?
- What equipment was on your trade-in that you would like on your new vehicle?
- Have you test-driven a vehicle?
- If there were one reason for you not to buy a new car right now, what would that reason be?
- Which of my vehicles could you see yourself owning?
- On a scale from 1 to 10, where 1 is that you leave without making a deal and 10 is that you buy the car right now, where on the scale would you say that you are? (Let's say the customers say "7.")
- What would it take for me to get you to 10?
- How long do you think it may take you to "think about it"? 2 weeks? 3 Weeks? Then the customers say "Oh no we are going to buy within "X" amount of time then go right into the 4 Ps.

### *A great close: the four P's*

*Person:* "I certainly hope I haven't offended you in any way. You'd buy a car from me, wouldn't you?" ("Oh no, when we get ready, we are buying from you.")

*Place:* "You'd buy from our dealership, wouldn't you?"

*Product:* "You did say you like the car well enough to own it, didn't you?"

*Price:* "Gosh, Mr. and Mrs. Customer, it seems you have found the salesperson you want to buy from, found the dealership you want to buy from, and found the right car you want to buy. Hmmm, let me guess: What you are going to think about is whether or not this makes sense in your budget. Am I correct?"

If they are looking for something in particular that you do not have, for instance, a specific color or equipment package, they must drive something similar while you figure the best switch unit, dealer trade, or order unit, in that sequence. Always make every effort to sell what you see rather than you see what you can sell.

Often, the managers must use F.O.R.M. (family, occupation, recreation, me) to open the customer. Most customers will easily open up to questions about their family, their recreational interest, their occupation, or themselves.

There are dozens of other questions managers can ask as well. Obviously, the T.O. happens at different stages of the process, and the managers' job is ultimately to continue the process with the customers.

6. **KISS: Keep it simple stupid.** The managers asking for the order is often enough to overcome the objection. Just make sure the customers are seated and their body language is right. Some people enjoy talking to the

managers and feel they got the best deal that way, even if the sales associates haven't presented an offer yet! Some customers are much less likely to say no to a manager.

Managers always hold gross better when they are in the habit of talking to all of the customers. Most dealerships have plenty of hard rules for the sales associates and *few*, if any, for the sales managers. It's time to make your managers personally manage the sales. The results will surprise you.

7. **Sales managers *must pay attention* and be cognizant of every deal, ready, willing, and able to jump into action.** The managers should constantly be making mental notes of things like the body language of both the sales associates and the customers. As remedial as this sounds, in the majority of the dealerships I go into, the managers are not paying attention to the lot or the showroom. It's likely that you assume this isn't a problem at your dealership.

Dealers with well-managed floors take sales managers who do not rely on the sales staff to manage themselves or the sales floor. They take sales managers who assist in the selling effort from the word *go*.

# CHAPTER 7

# The Salesperson Life Wheel

This chapter is based on a sales meeting that I give. It is something I teach all my salespeople, and it's the most significant thing that they will learn about making what they do into a career rather than just a job.

A lot of people get into the car business just to have work until they get a job in another field, until they get their degree and do this or that, until they start a business, or whatever. It's just a job.

In the car sales business, everyone is in one of the four stages of what I call the "sales life cycle." It's a fluid situation where you can go from one stage to the other, except Stage 4. Stage 4 is extremely difficult to get to. If you ever do get this stage, and very few do, it's very hard to slide back from there.

The following is an illustration of the four stages of the sales lifecycle.

## SALES LIFE CYCLE

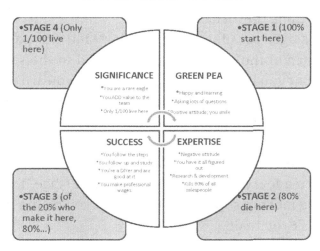

## Stage 1: Green Pea

Everyone in the retail automobile industry starts off in Stage 1. From dealer principals to salespeople, no one is excluded. When you are at this stage, you are what is affectionately called a "green pea."

When you are a green pea, you are enthusiastic, you are happy to have a job, and you want to revolutionize the car business. Everything is new to you, and you are excited to meet the customers. You are determined to be honest with them and change the general perception of car salespeople.

You don't know what you are doing, but you typically put a few Xs on the board – you sell a few cars – simply because you don't know the answers, so you ask a lot of questions. And you don't know the power of questions. You are also genuinely excited to meet people, and people feel and understand genuineness.

I'm a dog lover, and I have several dogs. If I go to the restroom in my house, and I come out of the restroom, my dogs attack me because they are so happy to see me again. They jump up and down and wag their tails like I have been gone to the war. I can tell that they genuinely love me.

As a green pea, you are happy to see customers. You are just excited to see people and go out and talk to them. All the negativity hasn't crept in yet, and all the other salespeople haven't told you about everything they feel is wrong.

At this stage, you don't quite understand the pay plan, the lingo, or much of the processes and the road to the sale. You are just green. But you have that positive attitude, you are excited, and you ask a lot of questions, and those three things are hard to beat.

You are also putting more Xs on the board than some of the people who have been there two years, three years, four years, and you think, "Gosh, this is easy."

You learn a lot when you are in the green stage. You typically listen during meetings, you take notes, and you do the things your managers ask you to do.

You don't get caught up in the negativity and the huddles about what is wrong. You just try to learn. Your mind is open, and the human mind is exactly like a parachute: it only works when it's open. It's a beautiful thing when you are a green pea.

The bad news is that your green pea stage comes to an end. Depending on your level of adaptation, your management, and a lot of other things, the green-pea stage can last anywhere from three months to three years. Then you get to Stage 2, which I have nicknamed "expertise."

## Stage 2: Expertise

Expertise is a moniker that I picked up from Jim Ziegler at Ziegler SuperSystems when I saw him at Norcross, Georgia, in the '90s.

This second stage kills about 80% of salespeople; it is the deadliest thing ever to befall us salespeople. Most don't make it through this stage.

When you get to Stage 2, you stop asking questions, and you start telling. Telling isn't selling. Telling is the anti-selling. No one can tell and sell. Everyone likes the feeling of buying something. Nobody likes the feeling of being sold or told something. How can you learn about people to open a deal if you don't ask questions?

At this stage, your percentage of conversions of customers who are looking into customers who are buying lowers a lot because you think you know it all now, so you are telling. You tell people what you think their trade is worth before the manager appraises it. You tell people they have negative equity without knowing what that means. You tell them what the invoice is, and you tell them what they can't do. *Can't* becomes a central word in your vocabulary when you are in expertise. You are quick to tell people: "Hey, don't buy things from the finance man in the back. You don't need that stuff." You are quick to tell them about interest rates before you have any idea what the customer qualifies for.. You don't know what holdback is, but you talk about that as well. (Holdback is a small percentage that the dealers make on each deal, and they typically don't pay salespeople on it.) You get negative.

You get on what I call the "Research and Development Committee." Sometimes you even become the chairperson of this committee, which is a group of salespeople who huddle and complain about everything they could possibly complain about. They complain about the inventory, the pay plan, the weather, the economy, the president, and the managers – all the reasons why they aren't selling enough cars. They externalize rather than internalize. They externalize everything and come up with ridiculous reasons for not selling cars. This stage afflicts dealers and managers too; it's an equal opportunity disease.

Say you are a salesperson in Stage 2, and you meet customers who tell you, "We're just looking," which is a reflex objection that 90% of customers say even if they come in to buy cars. Then, instead of saying your name and asking the customers the appropriate questions, like if they are there for current a sale, you just say, "What are you looking for?"

It's like if someone goes to the doctor and says, "I have a sore throat," and the doctor says: "Here's amoxicillin. Go home and take the medication." But the patient is allergic to amoxicillin, so when taking this medication, he or she asphyxiates and dies. The doctor is guilty of malpractice because he or she didn't ask any questions and check if the patient was allergic to amoxicillin. The doctor just decided to diagnose the patient with an infection and prescribe some of this medication, and it killed the patient.

Salespeople suffering through the expertise stage do the same thing. When customers tell a salesperson at this stage what they are looking for – if they, for example, say: "We're looking for a $6,000 to $8,000 car," the salesperson gets excited and says: "Oh, a $6,000 to $8,000 car? Hold on just a minute." Then this salesperson runs into the sales tower and excitedly tells the manager: "Hey, I've got some buyers who are looking for a $6,000 to $8,000 car. Do we have anything?" Typically, there are not a lot of $6,000 to $8,000 cars up front at most franchise dealerships; they are usually in the back on the trade row.

When the manager says that they have a couple of cars in that price range that they can show the customers, the salesperson runs out to the customers and takes them to see these cars. But when the customers see these cars, they are truly disgusted. Then the customers share something with the salesperson that the salesperson should have known: "What we're looking for is a car with leather interior, a sunroof, and navigation. We would prefer brand X, and we want less than 100,000 miles."

The expertise salesperson thinks that these people are idiots for wanting a leather interior, a sunroof, navigation, and less than 100,000 miles for $6,000 to $8,000. Then the salesperson tells the customers: "Here is my card. If I find anything like it, I'll call you" and shoos away the customer.

Then the salesperson runs back to the sales manager, and the sales manager agrees with the salesperson when he or she says: "Those customers were idiots. They wanted a $6,000 or $8,000 car with leather interior, a sunroof, navigation, and under 100,000 miles." The tragedy is that the sales manager agrees with the salesperson and says: "Get a real customer; I agree with you that these people are idiots."

Then a salesperson who is not in Stage 2 goes up to these customers, takes their hands, and introduces himself or herself. This salesperson asks what the customers' names are, what brought them out, if they are there to see anybody, or if they are there for the big sale. Then the customers say the same thing: "We're looking for a $6,000 to $8,000 car."

The salesperson then asks: "How are you going to pay for this car? Are you going to pay cash, write a check, borrow money from the bank, or take advantage of dealership financing?" The customers reply that they are looking for about $300 to $350 monthly payments. Now there are several vehicles with the equipment that they want in their payment range. There are likely a number of units on any given lot that would meet their criteria. The customers had equated the $6,000 or $8,000 to a $300 monthly payment. But now that this salesperson knows that it's a $350 payment, there are a lot of cars to show. Typically $350 turns into $450 so it might even be possible to get that payment with a new car on a purchase or lease.

When you are in Stage 2, and you don't ask any questions, you miss deals. The second salesperson, who is not in Stage 2, ends up making a deal with the customers, shaking hands, and getting customers for life. The Stage 2 salesperson thought that those customers were idiots, but the idiot is the salesperson in Stage 2.

Stage 2 salespeople always complain about the pay plan. They think they are getting cheated out of their commission and that the finance people are selling products behind their back and taking their money. Taking profit from the salesman to finance manager.

What always makes me laugh is when Stage 2 salespeople get upset and quit their job. They get interviewed at another dealership and get a job there. But they take their bad habits with them. They still don't follow up, and they still don't ask questions. Their mind remains closed.

Their green enthusiasm is gone. Now they have experienced indifference. And they will take that experienced indifference with them to other car lot and do nothing that they are supposed to do. Then they think they are going to be successful at the other lot, and they tell all the other salespeople and the managers there why they weren't successful where they were before. They say the dealership they were at previously doesn't appraise cars enough, doesn't advertise enough, doesn't have the right inventory, has got the wrong managers, has the wrong location, and so on.

Inevitably, they call the dealership they were at originally 30, 60, or 90 days later. It rarely passes 90 days, and it is unlikely to pass 60. Typically, around 45 days later, they call and say: "Hello, Mr. Sales Manager? Mrs. Sales Manager? This is Johnny Salesperson. Do you remember me? I sure miss you guys, and I want my job back. These people over here don't know how to do it like you do it. I'm behind on my rent, and I miss you guys. I made a big mistake leaving, and I want a second chance with you."

This happens because they have externalized their problems, and they went to the other dealership and took their bad habits with them there. Then they forgot how "bad" the dealership they quit was, and they try to come back. This happens over and over again.

When you are in Stage 2, it's a dark time. You badmouth your competition. You bad mouth your own co workers or dealership. You think that you are the most honest, hard-working person around and that the people you work with are liars and cheaters. You are quick to point out how bad everybody else is, especially the customers, management, owners, and people in the office.

At this stage, you don't follow up with the customers because you don't believe that works. You don't believe anything works, and you think you know it all. You say: "I heard about that whole positive attitude stuff, and I gave it a try for a day, but I knew it wasn't going to work." You are in a bad place, and you have a bad perspective on life. You are typically looking for other jobs and often dreaming of starting a business with your zero money in the bank. You hang out in small huddles complaining about everything.

You don't think to do things the way you are trained to do them, and you don't do anything the way you are supposed to. Still, you don't blame yourself.

Now you have been selling cars for eight months or a year, and you are not very successful at it. You are barely making a living. It's a bad situation because you are looking at the negatives. "That's not my job", or "I don't get paid for that" are common phrases of a stage 2 person.

Then green peas show up on the car lot, and they are happy, excited, and bright-eyed. They are going to make their follow-up calls, follow the scripts that the sales managers give them, and get online and get certified and learn everything they can about the cars.

The green peas follow the steps to the sale, and they do all the things that are necessary because they try to make the management and customers happy. They are excited, and they follow the steps. As a result, they are converting shoppers into buyers.

These green peas put Xs on the board – a lot more Xs than you do in Stage 2. Then you realize, "Something is going on here." You were convinced that cars wouldn't sell there, but now there are green peas who are selling more than you.

When you are in Stage 2, and green peas pass you, you think: "These green peas don't know what is wrong here. But they are going to find out when I get them alone and tell them. I can't believe they're selling that many cars. It's dumb luck. They don't know what they're doing."

You are upset that the green peas sell more cars than you, so you try to drag them down. You tell them what you think is wrong with the inventory, the advertising, the pay plan, the location, the managers, and everything else.

If the green peas don't listen to you, they will continue to sell cars, learn, and keep their minds open. They will listen during meetings, take notes, follow up with their clients, set appointments, ask questions, and follow the steps to selling cars. And you who are in Stage 2 recognize that. If you ever get past Stage 2 with all that negativity, you get into Stage 3.

## Stage 3: Success

Stage 3 is called "success." When you get to this stage, you have figured out that you need to learn how to smile even on bad days because when you were in Stage 2, you saw green peas selling cars, and you saw people who were in Stage 3 selling cars. And you saw that all of these people had one thing in common: The green peas were smiling, and the Stage 3s (successful salespeople) were smiling. You probably didn't see anyone at Stage 4. A lot of dealerships don't even have anyone at Stage 4 on the premises, but some of them do. Either way, you could tell that the people who were selling cars were asking questions and that they were smiling even when they were not happy.

A Stage 3 successful person understands the laws of attraction. Scientists have taught us that the laws of attraction exist.[13] If you smile, it causes others to smile. If you are happy, it causes people around you to be happier. If you have a bad and pushy attitude, and you push people emotionally, mentally, and verbally, then they are going to push you back. When you are in Stage 3, and you have reached success, you realize that, and you smile.

You also start asking questions. You realize that the people who invented the steps to the sale did that both to the advantage of the customers – to ease the customers' buying experience – and the salespeople. And you understand that the steps of the sale are very important.

You understand that if you follow up with your customers, text or call them and thank them for coming in, tell them what we have traded for, and get interested in them, they will get interested in you. It's mutually beneficial for the customers and you to follow up.

In Stage 3, the success is that you can do it yourself. You understand how to talk to the customers. You understand how to overcome the customers' fears. You understand how to make them feel better about dealing with you. You understand how to set them at ease. You understand how to help them better and how to assist

[13]    Watkins, E. R. (2008). Constructive and Unconstructive Repetitive Thought. *Psychological Bulletin, 134*(2), 163–206. http://doi.org/10.1037/0033-2909.134.2.163

them in buying a car. When you are in the success stage, rather than trying to sell somebody something, you understand how to help someone buy something. You help someone get something they need, or perhaps something they want.

At this stage, you see how important it is to set goals. You see how important it is to track yourself. You understand the intricacies of selling – that it's a profession to be learned. You read books, blogs, and articles, and you are learning and adding to your repertoire. You have learned heaps of words that are better than the words you used to have, and your toolbox of words has grown tremendously.

You understand how to overcome the seven or eight basic objections that most customers have. You understand how to build value in your car, and you understand how to explain the trade-in value of the customers' car.

You understand the deal structure a little bit. You also understand the bank financing and the payment structure. In addition, you have become a better communicator.

Most importantly, you have understood how essential your attitude is. It permeates throughout your entire deal, and your car deal starts to reflect that. What that means is that you are following the steps of the sale, and you are doing the things you are supposed to do. You are following the test drive route, and you are introducing your customers to the manager for the manager turnover.

Now you are making a good living. You have become a professional. You have survived Stage 2, which kills 80% of salespeople, and you have hit this success stage.

Here is another 80%-20% rule: If you hit the success stage, there is an 80% chance that you will be in sales for the rest of your life. You have arrived at a beautiful place, and you make professional wages. You are supporting your family in a professional manner. You probably live in a pretty nice home in a decent neighborhood, and you might be doing things that people in the upper middle class do.

Depending on what part of the country you are in, you could have a six-figure income. You could have a $150,000, or 200,000, or in some places $300,000 income. Or you could be in a community where $60,000 or $70,000 a year is a success. Either way, whatever success is where you are at, you have reached it, and you understand how to get there.

## Stage 4: Significant

The next stage is a very rare stage that I used to call the "eagle stage." Now I have changed the name of it to the "significant" stage, and I can credit John Maxwell with that terminology.

The difference between success and significance is that success is what you do for yourself; it's all about you while significance is what you do for others – what you do to make the team and dealership better, and what you do to add value to everything.

You make a difference to the team and would be missed if you were gone. When you are in the success stage, and you help a green pea or the next person to close the deal, you charge them half a deal. When you are at Stage 4, you help all the salespeople to close deals for free because you are glad to help them. When you see other salespeople going astray or struggling, you walk up to them and say: "Let me show you a better way." You are adding value to the entire dealership and the dealer's name.

When you reach the significant stage, everyone around you is better because you are there. It's in the little things you do: cheering up other people, noticing their attitude, and recognizing those who are suffering in the expertise stage and helping them see a better way to do things.

The people who are in the significant stage, Stage 4, are extremely rare. A lot of dealerships don't even employ a Stage 4 person. This person could be the general manager, a salesperson, or a finance person – anybody in the sales arena in the industry.

Many Stage 4 people prefer to be in sales rather than management because then they are not strapped to the dealership for 60 or 70 hours a week. They may have kids and may be going to ball games, or they may be volunteering. A lot of people in the significant stage are the type of people who would volunteer.

You see the big picture when you are in the significant stage. Rather than criticizing the green peas when they come in, like you may do when you are successful, you walk up to them and say: "I saw where you lost this customer. Let me show you a better way. This is a how you call your customers back, or this is what you say when you come back from a test drive. Allow me to show you some intricacies of CRM that will help you with inventory and your follow up. And let me show you a way that you can get the factory to pay you more money when you sell cars by being certified." At this stage, you teach it, you do it, and you live it.

You may not be the general manager or the manager performing the actual sales meetings, but you are a walking, talking, and breathing sales meeting. You are a leader. You know the way, and you go the way and show the way. You have reached a point where you make very good, professional wages, and the dealership would have a huge hole if you were gone. You uplift the entire dealership. You uplift the industry. You are a rare eagle.

I use birds as an example. Obviously, when you are a green pea, you are a young bird, and you are flapping around trying to learn how to fly. It's a time when you occasionally need others to put some worms in your mouth.

When you hit Stage 2, you are a turkey or a chicken. Chickens and turkeys peck each other's poop. Sometimes they follow each other around because they can't wait for the poop to hit the ground. When a rainstorm comes, some domesticated turkeys will look up in the air, and they will drown themselves. I grew up in the country, and I know it for a fact.

If you have survived Stage 2, then you hit Stage 3, and you are moving further ahead in the hierarchy of birds. Maybe you are a cardinal or a sparrow at this time. You go around and dig up worms, and you are at a place where you can make it.

When you hit Stage 4, and you are a significant, you are an eagle, and eagles don't hang out with turkeys and chickens. As a matter of fact, they will eat them if they get hungry. They don't hang out with cardinals and sparrows. Eagles fly on their own. Sometimes in a storm, rather than looking up and drowning themselves like a domesticated turkey, they will fly up above the clouds, and the storm won't affect them. I have yet to see a turkey and an eagle or a chicken and an eagle in the same picture. There is no such thing, even though they are all birds.

Let me caution you how quickly stages can change. One bad phone call where you get mad and upset can cause you to slide from Stage 3, success, to Stage 2. It is a fluid wheel where you can slide back and forth. But Stage 4 is hard to slide back from or too far out of. People at this stage are cognizant of which of these four stages they are in. That helps them to understand what they are going through, and it will help them not to die from expertise and become successful or significant.

# CHAPTER 8

# Avoiding Slumps

Every sales manager, every owner, and every salesperson selling anything in the world will, at some point, cross paths with the dreaded slumps. These slumps are mentally and economically taxing. They can also be taxing on your family. And they can be difficult to crawl out of.

Usually, you will encounter a slump pretty early. And you will likely face slumps – big and small – many times over. When you get into your very first slump, you will say: "This isn't for me. Maybe I should do something else."

In a world where bills are paid week-to-week, month-to-month, and day-to-day, any slump can have brutal implications. Very rarely are there any savings to dig into if you need them. And you have a tough time overcoming the slumps because you don't understand them. Then, when you don't have any money left, you think: "Oh, gosh. I'm living in a world of commission right now. I've got to pay my bills. I needed a steady paycheck." Then you panic.

Slumps are inevitable. If they are inevitable, you may wonder what you can do. In this chapter, I will show you 30 slump-busting techniques designed to help you steer clear of prolonged slumps completely or quickly jump out of them, so they don't ruin your career.

## 1. Get Back to the Basics

The primary common denominator for all sales slumps is that you have drifted away from the basics, and you are skipping steps. Going from first base to home plate only counts when all the bases are touched. If you don't touch all the bases, you don't have a run. The thought "This just isn't for me" goes hand in hand with abandoning the basics. Get reacquainted with the basics, and you will likely reacquaint yourself with deals.

## 2. Adjust Your Attitude

When you have a poor attitude, you are likely to be the last one to recognize it.

Even the great leaders I know say: "Roger, I'm struggling to keep my positive attitude." It takes work to keep your positive attitude. How often do you concentrate on having an attitude of gratitude for all that you have rather than worry about what you don't have, and working with what you have rather than wishing that you had something else?

As I said before, I believe the laws of attraction exist. A poor attitude rubs off on your customers, so it's essential that you give yourself a checkup every day – and sometimes several times a day – when it comes to your body language. You have to ignore negativity and permeate positivity. You have to smile even when it hurts and you don't feel like doing it.

If negativity is in your speech or body language, you have a serious illness. Looking for what is wrong is moving backward. Spending time thinking about what coworkers, bosses, dealers, or customers are doing wrong is sales suicide. Learn both positive speech and body language, and spend time practicing it.

## 3. Study Your Profession

Knowledge empowers you; it is KEY. Study your profession. Read or listen to motivational or sales related books. Listen during training meetings. Study as if you are studying for the biggest exam of your life. Entrench yourself in knowledge. Knowledge is a power that will propel you through the dreaded slump.

## 4. Balance Your Life

If your life is out of balance, you are driving your career with a wheel that is out of balance. It's a rough and bumpy ride that gradually gets worse.

Are you scheduling your time with your family and significant other? What about your you-time? Do you have hobbies you enjoy? How about your higher power? I know that when I'm right with God, my life feels a lot smoother.

Not making time for these things is a recipe for cooking up a prolonged slump. Make a schedule and stick to it. Working twice the hours is tempting in the competitive sales environment, but it's the road to nowhere. Keep your life in balance.

## 5. Have Fun

There is no shortage of practical jokers in our industry, and there is no harm in good-natured fun. Having fun with your prospects and your co-workers is healthy. Laughing customers are buying customers.

There is no need to go overboard with the fun. Keep the fun in its place, but eliminating the fun in sales is inviting the slump. You have to have fun. You have to have so much fun that if you didn't need money to live in this world, you would do this job for free.

## 6. Accept Responsibility

When you realize that you are falling into a slump, you might begin playing the blame game. The blame game makes it difficult to move forward. "If we had more or different inventory, I'd make more money. If my manager would listen to me more, I'd make more money. At the store I worked at before, we had better processes. Our advertising doesn't work."

You get worried about fixing the dealership, but don't worry about all that. Fix yourself. It's not complicated. When you are on the Research and Development Committee trying to fix everything else, you are always losing because you are not focusing on what you are supposed to focus on, and you are headed straight to Slumpville.

## 7. Questions Are the Answer

No one cares how much you know until they know how much you care. You have to ask questions before you give your diagnosis. You need to put in the time to understand where your customers are coming from and what their actual needs are.

After we have been selling for a while, we become experts, and we begin telling instead of selling. Telling is not selling; it's the formula for anti-selling.

Don't forget to ask your prospects the necessary fact-finding questions, and then listen to their answers. Ask more and listen more. Answer questions with questions. Listen between the lines.

## 8. Can't Never Could

*Can't* is a word that is at the forefront of the vocabulary of most sales associates who are mired in a slump. They will even say: "Let me see if I can't do this. Let me see if I can't get that much for your trade." They will tell the customer: "You can't get that price. You can't get that payment. You can't do this. You can't do that."

Telling customers what they can't do is poor salesmanship. There are only two *can'ts* in the sales business: If you can't sell, you can't stay. Always tell the customers what you can do and what they can do, and then ask for the order. You will find this is a magic slump killing medicine.

## 9. Get Inspired

Did you choose this profession due to a need to make an income greater than that of an hourly or salaried position? What inspired you to be in sales? Was it a nice home, a lot of toys, or the lifestyle? Was it your family security? Was it your kids? Was it a chance to start over in life? Whatever inspired you to sell, concentrate on that inspiration. It's a natural repellent for slumps.

## 10. Overcome Fear

FEAR stands for false events appearing real. Fear is not real, but it's real powerful. Fear creates slumps out of thin air. You may have a fear of asking closing questions, a fear of failure, or a fear of rejection. Perhaps you think: "Everybody is watching me, and I can't get my customers to do anything." You shut down because you become fearful. Fear is a slump creator. Boldly do what you have been taught to do, and do so with enthusiasm.

## 11. Talk to Your Mentor

All successful salespeople have had other successful salespeople train, inspire, or coach them along the way. No one became successful on their own.

Use your support group of winners rather than huddle with losers who are making excuses. Get back on track with the people at the top, not the bottom. Turkeys and chickens – people in Stage 2 – stand around at the bottom and peck each other's poop, but eagles don't do that. Get off on your own. Talk to your mentor, talk to an eagle, not a turkey. If you are always the most successful person in your crowd, it's time to change crowds.

## 12. Don't Give Up

More often than not, the breakthrough is just around the corner. Selling is like riding a bicycle; you have to keep moving. The business is full of extreme highs and extreme lows. Don't live in either for prolonged periods, and let neither one of those define you. Einstein said: "It's not that I'm so smart, it's just that I stay with problems longer."[14] If Einstein didn't give up easily, then neither should you.

---

[14]   *Albert Einstein quote.* (n.d.). Retrieved December 14, 2015, from
       http://www.brainyquote.com/quotes/quotes/a/alberteins106192.html

## 13. Enthusiasm Is the Potion That Creates Motion

"For every sale you miss because you're too enthusiastic, you will lose a hundred because you're not enthusiastic enough."[15] That is some more of Zig Ziglar's wisdom.

Film your presentation. How do you look? How does it sound to you? Would you buy from you? Listen to yourself on the phone. How do you sound? Be a commercial. Excitement sells. Do you sound distracted? Do you answer your cell phone when you are talking to customers? Are you tired, depressed, or angry? Are you uninspired? All these are ingredients for a slump. Get back to enthusiasm.

## 14. List Your Goals and Read Them Aloud Daily

Every morning, write down your goals and read them aloud. It seems nearly impossible to get salespeople to do this. It seems so simple that maybe the power of it escapes us.

Perhaps you think: "I know my goals, so why should I write them down every day?" For starters, the difference in the level of success of people who do write down goals and the people who don't is a mile wide. The power of writing down your goals is greater than what I can describe. It's slump vaccine on steroids, so write them down every day, read them aloud, and see what that does to your slump.

## 15. Get Karma on Your Side

Focus on being inspirational rather than critical. Do more than your share to assist the team effort. Rather than thinking about what is in it for you, help other people reach their goals.

Be a person who would be missed if you were gone. Don't be the person who says, "That is not my job." Be a person who does little things that aren't in the job description. Be a person

---

[15]   *Zig Ziglar quotes.* (n.d.). Retrieved December 14, 2015, from http://thinkexist.com/ quotation/for_every_sale_you_miss_you-re_too_enthusiastic/145444.html

who takes pride in the work, is positive to be around, and helps everyone. If someone else has a good idea or does a good job, give credit where it is due; it doesn't have to be your idea or something you did.

Criticism and selfishness are slump magnets. There are many people around who are selfish and like to criticize. Don't be one of them.

## 16. Don't Outrun Your Resume

Don't get ahead of your resume. What you used to do doesn't matter. The Bible tells the story of what happened to Lot's wife as they were leaving Sodom and Gomorrah. An angel told her not to look back, but she did, and she turned into a pillar of salt. Don't look back like her.

No one cares what you used to do. It's that simple. Leave the past in the past, and let's talk about the now and the future. The questions are: What have you done lately? How many units have you or your department sold right now?

Clinging on to what you used to do or how you used to do it, or trying to relive the good old days prevents you from moving forward into today's good times.

## 17. Keep Your Eye on the Ball

Focus may sound so simple that it deserves no mention, but far from it. Lack of focus is prevalent amongst salespeople. Wasted time is the companion of low production.

It's amazing to me how many people are not selling anything, but still they are doing all kinds of things that serve no purpose in selling cars. They have lost focus. Why would you not be doing something to create a deal rather than focusing on things guaranteed not to create a deal?

# 18. Go All In

Lose the mentality of "I guess I'll do this until I get a real job." Stop looking around for other jobs instead of learning this one. Giving a half-hearted effort to sales is self-inflicted mental abuse. This is a very difficult job if you don't go all in.

If you want to be more successful in sales, and you want to avoid the slumps, then you must sell out completely. This is who I am. This is what I do. I'm going to be the very best at it.

Even if it didn't make your parents proud when you got into the car business, even if you never dreamt you would be in sales, you have to be very proud of who you are and what you do.

Many average salespeople try to start their own business or jump to another job without studying the best practices of the job they have. They just learn a little bit of it and then they go looking for something else. You have to sell out and learn everything about this job. Without 100% commitment, this isn't going to work.

## 19. Avoid Playing the Victim

This is no business for the self-pitying crowd. In the auto sales business and sales in general, you get paid what you are worth. Remember Winnie the Pooh? Remember his self-pitying friend Eeyore? This business doesn't fit the Eeyores of the world, the woe-is-me or why-me crowd.

Victims and the thin-skinned are out of this business more quickly than you can say lickety-split. The victim card is easy to play, and it's a bad habit to get into. Stay away from this deadly sales career killer.

## 20. Avoid Gossip

Sales floor gossip is a real momentum breaker. It seems harmless to listen to or even join in. But the truth is that if you do, you always end up mired in drama, even if you are not the one doing the gossiping.

It has been proven that secondhand smoking can kill you, and it has killed people. Secondhand drama will kill your sales career. If your words are not inspiring or uplifting, they are grave digging, and eventually you will fall into the pits they dig, whereas if your words are uplifting, they will lift you up. All people are elevators; we can bring people up or take them down. Don't take people down because you go with them.

Gossip is like your shadow. You can't run fast enough to get away from it because it's your dark reflection. Slumps are best friends of gossip. You rarely see one without the other.

## 21. Have an Outlet

Whether you express yourself in music, weightlifting, yoga, running, or a myriad of other things, you must do something to release negativity and stress.

Successful salespeople are conduits for taking in negativity and putting out positivity. Releasing this negativity is a must. When people ask me why so many older salespeople are negative, the simple answer is that they have retained too much negativity over the years.

During your career, certain customers will treat you poorly and even say rude or unnecessary things to you. Face it: Car salespeople are easy targets. You must not take it personally, react to it, or return the bad behavior. Professionals specialize in returning poor behavior with positivity.

## 22. Be Prepared

Arrive at work prepared to do business. Preparation is a many-splendored blessing when you do it, and it's a curse when you don't. "It's not the will to win that matters – everyone has that. It's the will to prepare to win that matters."[16] That is a quote by Bear Bryant, and I love it.

---

[16]    Roberts, D. (2012, August 7). *Top 50 quotes from Bear Bryant*. Retrieved December 14, 2015, from http://www.saturdaydownsouth.com/2012/bear-bryant-50-quotes/

My old coach used to tell us that proper preparation prevents poor performance. We all know the salesperson who is always 10 minutes late, can't find a pen, has wrinkled clothes, and has few sales as a result.

What are you doing to be well prepared? The well prepared seem to find deals through muddy waters. Slumps hide from the well prepared like thieves hide from law enforcement.

## 23. Smile

If you see someone without a smile, give that person your smile. There is no magic like the magic of a contagious smile. People will mirror their company, and a sourpuss expression is not what you want from your customers.

If you have troubles at home or wherever, put them in an imaginary bag and set them on the curb when you pull into the dealership. Don't share them with anybody because when you leave, those problems will still be there. No one wants your problems. While you are in the sales environment, remember to smile as if you don't have a care.

## 24. Be Honest

Everyone deserves honesty, including you. The lies that we tell ourselves are the most damaging. Lying to customers and coworkers leads to lack of credibility and production, and eventually it leads to job-hopping. You will be surprised by how being honest with everyone will help you get out of the slump. One of my favorite jokes is, "I'm the most honest salesperson ever. I wouldn't lie, cheat, or steal, but those people I work with, you have to watch them."

Knowing everyone deserves honesty; give it to them even when they don't give it to you. You don't have t say all you know in every situation, but you do have to keep it real.

## 25. Stop Running for Mayor

The classic examples of people who are "running for mayor" are those who consistently recite their resume to their peers. They never miss an opportunity to verbalize their contributions, and they have the habit of exaggerating their efforts and taking undeserved credit.

Reciting a real or exaggerated past of accomplishments like a broken record is a bad thing. For example, sales managers always telling the salespeople how many cars they used to sell when they were on the sales floor doesn't help anybody sell cars.

The mayors, as I named these people years ago, are quick to point out anything that goes wrong yet shuck any responsibility: "That wasn't my deal. That was before I started working here." They are quick to say, "I got that deal bought," "I bumped the lender," etc., while they rarely give credit where it is due.

Stop running for mayor. Let's just get the job done.

## 26. Walk Around the Building Backward

This is my personal favorite. In my career, hundreds of sales associates and sales managers have contacted me saying: "Roger, after a week with no sales, I can't believe it. I walked around the building backward, just like you told me to, and I sold four cars in two days."

Walking around the building backward is an old salesperson slump-killing remedy. Some will laugh or scoff at it, but it is the single most effective method I have ever tried. You must walk around the whole building backward. You may try changing your alarm clock to an earlier wake-up time, your typical daily routine, and other habits as well. However, the backward walk is most important. Somehow, this changes the mojo and causes your ebb to become a flow.

## 27. Keep Your Pipeline Full

The batter's box, the on-deck circle, and the dugout must be loaded with potential hitters. The salesperson who is skilled in keeping the pipeline full is very skilled at avoiding slumps.

Those pipeline deals tend to come together all at once. I've always said selling is like fishing; it seems like they are all biting or none of them are biting. If you leave gaps in your pipeline, you will have gaps in your sales, so you must care for the pipeline constantly.

If you master the skill of setting appointments, you will guard yourself against slumps. Appointments are the best medicine for slumping sales. Typically, even a terribly slumping salesperson cannot keep a consistent appointment flow from creating sales. Appointments sell cars.

## 28. Network

Networking is important because the more people who know you and know what you do, the more potential clients you will have. Talk to businesses, individuals, churches, sports teams, bars, and so on. Wherever you go, network. Let all your friends, neighbors, and acquaintances know who you are and what you do.

## 29. Market Yourself

There are very many social media sites and business sites these days. It's a wise decision to invest in marketing yourself. By marketing yourself, you will get opportunities you would not have received through any other means.

Converting opportunities you would not have had otherwise is invaluable when avoiding the dreaded slumps. There is a lot you can do with Facebook, YouTube, etc., and branding your name with a hashtag and coming up with a nice little logo or slogan. Get involved with e-commerce today.

## 30. Fake It Until You Make It

Don't feed the slump with any form of verbalization because doing so tends to enhance the slump's foothold. You must pretend everything is fine and act as if you closed and delivered the last 100 prospects you spoke with.

These 30 slump busters I've shared with you will assist you to make money and keep your sanity because they will help you avoid or jump out of the dreaded slumps. Knowing how to avoid and escape these slumps can be the difference between failure and success.

CHAPTER 9

# Selling with a Servant's Heart

In this chapter, we will look at managing and selling with a servant's heart. It's very important that you understand this culture. A sales department that is led by a person who sells with a servant's heart is much better than any other. If serving is beneath you, leadership is beyond you.

Let that sink in for a minute:

*If serving is beneath you, leading is beyond you.*

You have to take it upon yourself to understand what it is to sell with a servant's heart. When you sell with that attitude, you take all the selfishness and shortsightedness out of it.

Perhaps you think, "What's in it for me right now? Why should I be nice to these customers who aren't going to buy a car right now? Why should I do anything to help out around here? If the bathroom needs toilet paper, why should I care? I use a different bathroom. The new people, why should I help them?" If this is the way you think, you will never reach Stage 4, significance.

## Bottom-Up Culture Versus Top-Down Culture

I call it a bottom-up culture versus a top-down culture. In a bottom-up culture, the salespeople serve the sales managers; the sales managers serve the general managers; and the general managers, general sales managers, and executive managers serve the owners. That is how most dealerships operate, and that is wrong.

The dealer is at the top. He or she has the greatest responsibility, and God has given this person a great opportunity. The owner or dealer should serve the general manager, the general sales manager, and the executive managers. The executive managers, general managers, and general sales managers should serve their sales managers. The sales managers should serve the salespeople, and all of them should serve the public – the customers.

If you are a general manager or dealer at a dealership, and you say: "I don't talk to the customers because I'm the ultimate authority, and they're just going to ask me for stuff," then you have got it all wrong. You have to show the way. John C. Maxwell said: "A leader is one who knows the way, goes the way, and shows the way."[17] As a leader, you have to serve the public by showing everyone else how to do it.

If a customer is upset or doesn't understand something, you need to speak with that customer. Turn the culture upside down. Instead of a bottom-up culture, have a top-down culture. Take a lot of your pride out of it. Have more empathy. Understand where everybody is coming from, and help them.

Learn how to deal with dishonest management or salespeople and unruly or dishonest customers effectively.

We create management opportunities, but we don't create leadership. Selling with a servant's heart is what leadership is all about. If you are a true leader, you understand a servant's heart. You pick up the trash you see on the lot. You don't leave anything unlocked or messy. When you see things that need fixing, you fix them. You don't criticize people and talk down to them. You take them by the hand and show them the way. You don't just point the way and tell them what to do. When you have what we call a lot party, where you rearrange the lot, and it's hot or cold outside, you are right there with the others. You shake the customers' hands with them.

When you have a servant's heart and lead from the front, it rubs off on everyone. The habit of going the extra mile always pays off. It might not be in your first paycheck, but it makes you who

---

[17]   *John C. Maxwell quote.* (n.d.). Retrieved December 14, 2015, from http://www.brainyquote.com/quotes/quotes/j/johncmaxw383606.html

you are and shapes how people think of you and how you think of yourself. It's about giving that extra bit, helping everyone else, and understanding what it takes to get people where they want to go and help them get there.

If you have a servant's heart, you don't ask what everyone can do for you. You reverse it, and you ask: "What can I do to help them? How can I add value to them? How can I add value to myself?"

## Stop Stealing

When I have sales meetings, and I train sales associates, one thing that I ask everybody to do is stop stealing. Some will stare at me like with an expression of, "Oh, God, you caught me." Most of them, however, will say: "I'm not a thief. I've never stolen anything." Stealing may or may not be an accurate word, but if sales associates ignore following up with their customers, they have a selfish attitude, and they are not selling from a servant's heart. They are stealing from their own commissions.

Also, would it be stealing if sales associates skip the steps to the sale? Yeah, I'm pretty sure it would. They are not selling from servants' hearts. Would it be stealing if they don't enter their clients into the CRM (Customer Retention Management)? Would it be stealing if managers don't train their associates? Would it be stealing not to drive in the trade? I certainly think a case can be made for these examples. If you sell or manage from a servant's heart, you won't do this.

There are a few basic laws of selling that are criminal to ignore. When I say stop stealing, what I'm saying is don't break the basic laws of selling. Based on my knowledge of the large percentage of sales associates that I have trained in 41 states in the United States and the six provinces in Canada that I have been to, I can tell what needs to be improved.

You can tell what needs to be improved about a dealership almost as soon as you walk in. Most are quick to say that the times have changed, the inventory has changed, the people have changed, and the advertising has changed. They will tell you everything that is wrong as soon as you walk in to talk to them. But very few ever think of changing themselves and selling from and living with a servant's heart.

They tell you their needs and ignore the obvious, which is that they need to change their negative attitude and obtain more skills. They need to prepare for success and chart and track the work. They need to increase their enthusiasm. They need to get to work on time. They need to practice and develop their skills, and they need to utilize these.

They need to improve their knowledge of the inventory and the products, and they need to improve the quality and quantity of their follow-up, their negotiation skills, and their focus on fixing sales. That is selling from a servant's heart.

If your ability to understand people isn't as good as you would like it to be, the cause may be that you don't value others as highly as you could. As you interact with people, remember the words of Ken Keys Jr.: "A loving person lives in a loving world. A hostile person lives in a hostile world: Everyone you meet is your mirror."[18]

## A Curious Cycle

I have been able to witness a rather curious cycle. It's perpetual in nature, yet it's new to each generation of car salespeople. It's the dynamic of meshing the new with the old that takes place every day on every sales floor.

Every generation of new car salespeople despise the old sales dogs, and the sales dogs laugh at the newbies. The youngsters have little respect for the old-fashioned dinosaurs roaming the sales floors. They understand the modern technology, and they are convinced that they have new and better ideas. The old sales

---

[18]    *A quote by Ken Keyes Jr.* (n.d.). Retrieved December 14, 2015, from http://www.goodreads.com/quotes/331046-a-loving-person-lives-in-a-loving-world-a-hostile

dogs ridicule the youngsters for their lack of understanding of the sales processes that work. In some ways, they are both right and in some ways, they are both wrong.

When I started out in car sales, I was a green pea full of energy and life, and I was determined that I was not going to be a car salesman like "those old dinosaurs." I looked at those guys, and I thought they couldn't do what I could do. I was going to be very different from them; I wasn't going to be rude to people or pressure them into buying cars they couldn't afford. I was determined to be honest, just like every new salesperson.

It was the early '90s, and I was a pretty strapping young man. I was 6-foot-2 and 200 pounds, and I was working out all the time, so I was in great shape. I was ready to tackle the world, and I was here to teach them a lesson. After all, I looked at those guys, and they were mostly lazy and overweight smokers. They were old, and they were dressed old fashioned. They would wear that old cologne that I couldn't stand. And they were constantly being smart alecks to their customers and other associates. They just seemed shady and uncaring to me, and I wasn't going to be like them. I was determined to beat them. I didn't respect them, and I let them know that. I had absolutely no idea that I had underestimated them because I was so full of myself.

I knew my customers were going to like me because I was going to be completely transparent and honest, and I was going to make all of them happy through hard work. Like so many before me, I was going to revolutionize the car sales business.

I was hired together with a dozen or so other green peas. Three of us – a guy named Tom, a guy named Mike, and I – made it beyond the first 90 days. I sold a vehicle from the lot for full window price to the very first customer I talked to, and I thought, "This is too easy."

From then things got a little tougher. Soon, I realized that I was taking a lot of ups (customers) and going on more test-drives than anyone else. I was working the hardest. Within a few weeks, my weight dropped down to 180 or so.

I was completely honest with my customers, and I was doing everything possible to please them. However, though I had seen a lot of customers, my sales were meager. A veteran on the lot said to me: "You're burning ups, boy. You won't last long in this business."

The others at the lot were laughing at what I did. Instead of having the customers follow me through our inventory, I would follow them around, which is a no-no in the car business. I was the one who should have known the cars rather than be shown the cars. When we would get back from test drives, my customers would promise to come back, but they didn't. It happened time and time again.

The older guys were making fun of me, and I was feeling the pressure. I got embarrassed, and I got desperate, so I started working double shifts, working 10, 12, and 14 hours a day. I was working so hard that I got exhausted mentally. I even found a used car cost sheet in the sales office and told my customers the cost of the cars.

My new car close was: "If I could sell it to you at invoice minus the rebates, would you buy it?" But nothing worked. Desperate selling isn't effective. It doesn't work. I didn't understand that. I was making them the best deal. Either the customers didn't believe me, or the lowest price wasn't selling cars for me.

Soon I fell into the trap of thinking that we had the wrong inventory. I thought that my managers didn't give enough for trades, and I thought that the cars were cheaper at other car lots and that our cars were too expensive. Most of all, I believed that my customers would come back. That is a prevalent thing that every green pea salesperson goes through.

My sales managers would ask me: "How many cars did you sell today? How many did you sell yesterday?" I would reply: "Oh, I sold none today, but I'm going to sell two tomorrow, Boss." The next day, I would say the same thing. My two never showed up. The old dinosaurs, however, kept marking Xs on the board, and they kept collecting commission money.

My team leader, who had closed most of the deals that I had made so far, taught me how to follow up, and soon I was acclimated to the "Oh-you-did club." The Oh-you-did club goes like this: You dial the phone and say: "Hi, is this Mr. and Mrs. Customer? This is Roger at ABC Motors. Oh. Oh, you did?" That "oh, you did" means they have bought a car somewhere else. All my customers who had promised me they would come back and wouldn't buy from anybody but me bought their car elsewhere. Most of the time, they made a deal with someone else the same day or the following day after having been at my dealership, which stunned me.

I couldn't believe these people were lying to me like that. They all told me they were going to buy from me. Many thanked me for not pressuring them, and they made all these promises to buy from me when they were ready. They said they just weren't ready yet. But they had lied to me, all of them. At first, I was angry with them for lying to me, and I thought: "I'll just treat them the way they treat me," but my conscience wouldn't allow me to do that. Then I witnessed something that made the light come on and make everything crystal clear, and it has never gone out since.

I had started working at the lot in February, and several months later, during the Memorial Day weekend, we were having a sale. As the sale was going on, I observed Bobby Crough, our used car manager at Lynn Hickey Dodge. He spoke with about a dozen customers over this three-day period. I watched him and listened to him as he spoke to these customers.

His customers had the same objections that my customers had, and they verbalized them exactly the same way. However, when they said: "We're just going to think about it, but we'll be back," he politely explained to them the advantages of buying then rather than leave. He made it make sense to them. He masterfully turned their objections and fears into warm fuzzy feelings. As a result, not only did they buy a car, but they also thanked him, and they were truly happy.

I was amazed. From then on, I became a student of the game, and I started reading Zig Ziglar, Joe Girard, Jim Ziegler, Joe Verde, Grant Cardone, and many others. I would also ask my friend Dave Anderson questions.

I learned that people wouldn't buy what you sold. They would buy what you believed. I learned that an extremely high percentage of people would fib regarding money. It didn't make them bad people. It made them human. It was a defense mechanism they used to protect their assets.

I learned that people wanted to feel good about decisions they made. That good feeling did not stem from agreeing with them when they were in a defense-mechanism mode. After all, if I agreed with them when they were fibbing to me, what would that make me? Did it make me the co-fibber or the fib enabler? Of course, it did. I was a fib enabler rather than a salesperson. Agreeing with them to make the decision to leave and think about it rather than buy from me right then was stupid.

I soon learned to sell the feel good. I had thought the customers would get the feel good when I offered them the lowest price and showed them the invoice and the used car costs. But they didn't.

I learned how to sell me, sell the dealership, sell the product, sell the finance, sell the trade value, sell the value of buying locally, and sell urgency. I sold from a servant's heart. I listened between the lines, and I discerned when they wanted a $14,000 car at $300 per month rather than the $6,000 car they had asked for.

I learned to ask the customers questions that brought out the map to the gold right out of their mouths. The more they told me about themselves, the more we bonded and the more I learned. Now I eagerly awaited their objections.

When Bobby Crough introduced himself to people, he didn't immediately start asking them for the sale. He immediately started asking them questions, and that was how he made sure they were in a car that they liked. I learned how to ask those questions and

SYNERGISTIC SELLING  Roger Williams

field their objections with ease. More importantly, I learned how to turn their fear into comfort. The customers wanted a salesperson they liked, but they wouldn't buy just because they liked me. They wanted a salesperson who would make them feel good about making a decision.

I used to let them choose to make no decision at all when they fibbed to me and reassured me that they would be back. When I smiled and agreed with them, I was oblivious to what they needed, and I sent them down the road to buy a car from someone else. They liked me, but I did not overcome their fear. I fed into it. I had been a great dummy, and many of us do what I had done.

Customers won't buy if they don't like you, but they won't buy just because they like you. You have to be able to sell the feel good. People don't want to be sold a car. They want help buying a car. They need you to help them. I had to learn to earn their respect and ask for the order. It was a revelation to me.

Just three months into the business, I had learned a lot about human nature. Originally, I had thought the steps to the sale were nonsense. I had sold some cars without following them. But eventually, I realized they were very powerful when they were followed. Buying a car was a magical experience, and it had to be treated as such. I had to learn to put the magic in it.

Now I'm 48 years old, and I have been making six figures for over 20 years. I have been there and done that. As a record-setting salesperson, F&I manager, used car manager, new car manager, general sales manager, general manager, and platform general manager, I have, in some ways, evolved into that dinosaur that I so resented when I was a green pea. But I'm thankful to Bobby Crough and Milton Moore, who taught me, and I'm paying forward their teaching every day.

I'm also still partly that energetic country boy who wants to revolutionize the auto industry by making customers love and trust me. I'm committed to training and coaching and teaching dealers, salespeople, and sales managers the best practices to grow them personally and professionally.

What I had to learn through observation and trial and error, I now teach every day from a servant's heart, and it brings me joy. I'm willing to jump right up there and help them.

One sales associate, one meeting, and one conversation at a time, I am revolutionizing our reputation as car salespeople. It's my goal to add value to every salesperson, every sales manager, every dealer, every vendor, and every customer I meet. The people who are winning understand the importance of adding value to their people and teaching them.

I don't smoke cigarettes and pitch quarters and make fun of green peas. I'm not rude or disrespectful to my customers. If I say I'm going to do something, I do it. If I promise something, I deliver it.

Over the years, I have probably spent $40,000 or $50,000 of my own money to buy extra keys or spare tires, or to fix a stereo knob or purchase some other item for my customers. If I recently sold a car, and the customers come back and claims that I said something, and I know I didn't say it because I say the same thing every time, I don't argue. I just accommodate them if they aren't rude. I do it every time.

I follow up religiously. I don't make people feel bad if they are currently too credit-challenged to buy a car. I'm not rude to buyers who are defensive or standoffish. I'm not rude if I feel like they are fibbing to me.

I'm very kind to green peas. I often laugh to myself at their innocence, rather than laugh at them. I especially get tickled when they agree with their customers that it's the right thing to do when they leave to think about it, even when the customers are in the defense-mechanism mode. That dynamic is one you have to experience before you accept it. The green peas try to sell me on the fact that their customers are coming back. I advise them of what I know, and I say that they shouldn't pressure people, just ask them a lot of questions and let them answer. I teach them to be honest and true to their word and themselves. Everybody deserves honesty. I get a thrill out of watching them grow as human beings and sales associates and knowing that they can support their family better and that their customers are getting a better experience.

As the entry-level dinosaur I know I have become, I still have a lot to learn, but I can assure you that the imprint I'm leaving on this business is better than the one I inherited. The lasting impression I'm leaving on the customers is one of the sales professional who cares.

In some strange ways, I'm still trying to prove to those old dinosaurs that there is a better way. I'm living it every day, one sales associate and one customer at a time.

# CHAPTER 10

# Closing the Deal, Growing and Cultivating Your Own Closers

In the last chapter, I talked about Bobby Crough, who was a used car manager at the great Lynn Hickey Dodge. Bob was and is a brilliant closer. He taught all the salespeople at Lynn Hickey Dodge, including me, how to paint word pictures. Some people might say they have a 14-ounce steak, but Bobby would say he had 14 ounces of mouth-watering USDA prime beef just dripping off the bone. When he sold a warranty, he didn't just tell the customers that it was a warranty. He told them it was a parts and labor agreement, and he told them about the rising costs of automobile repair.

Bob would also tell a story about some people he knew who had been traveling through a small town in Texas when their vehicle had broken down. There had happened to be an ASE certified mechanic in town, so they had gotten their car fixed, and they had gotten their hotel room and their towing covered. They had been up and running the next day, and they had only had to pay a $100 deductible.

When Bob sold appointments over the phone, he would say: "Your best leverage is your presence here. I have an opening at 2 PM and 3:30 PM, which one works best for you?" He would ask: "So how long do you think you are going to need to think about this, a day, a week, two weeks?"

He would tell us to draw and doodle on the worksheet, ask questions, and write down the answers. He would also say: "Open the deal, and then ask for the order. You have to be able to do that to be a closer. Everything you do is a step closer to the big yes!"

If the economy gets tough, the dealerships that will continue to do well are the ones with the best people. The best people have to be closers.

I have seen some great authors and some excellent trainers who failed to grasp the importance of closing. If you only focus on closing, you are wrong, but the closer is to the sales business what the thoroughbred is to horses.

You have to learn to recognize potential closers. You also have to learn how to develop them and reward them for being good or great closers.

## How to Find Good Closers

All managers and dealers want top-notch closers in their organization, but great closers are not going to show up ready made on your doorstep. If they are already good closers, they probably already have their own business. So if you want closers, then make a plan and grow your own rather than trying to recruit them from elsewhere by overpaying them. There are potential closers everywhere. When we see that potential in people, we have to grow them. Closing is an art born of passion; there is no such thing as passionless closers.

Unfortunately, managers and dealers usually have no idea how to detect great closers. To find potential closers, the first thing I recommend doing is implementing a liner-closer system. I believe in this system, and I think that every dealership should implement it. No salesperson should be sent out to deal with customers after just a week or a few days' worth of training. New hires should be put on a team with a veteran salesperson who understands how the job works.

Once you have put this system in place, you observe your salespeople. Who is excited about going into the deal? Who is willing to take the time to learn how to open the deal so that they can close it? Who is almost immune to rejection? These are some of the characteristics you look for in potential closers.

SYNERGISTIC SELLING  Roger Williams

Perhaps they are not well dressed, and they might not be the first ones to get to work. They may even have a tendency to want to skip things. But if you see that they are great with the customers, they are capable of getting them to see things their way, they talk to every one of them, and they have a positivity that is hard to overcome, then they have the potential to be a closer. The closers are the people who believe beyond a shadow of a doubt that they are going to make it happen. It's like a light.

Recognizing closing ability is paramount if you want to have closers. You need to monitor, observe, and track opportunities.

## How to Develop Good Closers

When you see these positive traits add up in people, then you need to invest more time and training to make them into professional closers. If you want to cultivate closers, you have to train every manager and every salesperson every day. This training happens in formal training sessions with the entire team, in one-on-one training sessions, and with customers. That is how you create your own breeding ground.

You teach them how to open the deal and overcome objections – not just the primary six or seven common ones but also secondary and tertiary ones. Teach them how to have tough conversations. It's okay to disagree with someone as long as you say it right and don't make it into an argument or debate.

Closers also need to learn how to ask the professional questions. Someone told me a long time ago: "The only difference between a loser and a closer is a *C*, and you have to find your *C*." Most people are afraid to ask the tough questions. That fear gets in the way and stymies their minds. Then they don't become a student of the game.

People tend to focus on closing the deal, and that ruins the close. As I said earlier, nothing can close until it's open. Great closers must be great openers, so you have to teach them the techniques of opening the sale.

The following are characteristics of good closers.

**Outward appearance.** A professional closer shows up to work well groomed and well dressed – sharp looking –every day. A closer looks important, and you can tell this person is a professional.

**Attitude and passion.** Good closers are charismatic people with award-winning smiles and can-do attitudes. They are consistent in what they say and do, and they give maximum effort each day. They understand the power of positivity, and they find something positive in any situation. They never get down, regardless of how things are going – how a month, a week, or a particular sale is going. They do it with passion. You can't teach passion.

They are the ones who the customers remember. If the customers come back in, they may say: "Hey, we bought this car from Roger," but Roger was not the salesperson; he was the closer.

When you sell from a servant's heart, it creates a sincerity that is characteristic of closers. John Wooden, my favorite coach of all time, said: "Things work out best for those who make the best of the way things work out."[19] I have always loved that quote.

Politeness, professionalism, and kind words are other characteristics of closers. They use what is called a velvet hammer.

All great closers have to act as conduits; they take in negative energy and put out positive energy. They are not afraid of rejection, and very rarely do you see a great closer get angry or become confrontational. They possess the virtue of patience. If you don't have patience, you can't be a closer.

They also need to have a sense of humor; they must be witty enough to laugh at themselves. Laughing customers are buying customers.

Good closers can make decisions without second-guessing themselves, and they would rather ask for forgiveness than permission.

---

19 *A quote by John Wooden.* (n.d.). Retrieved December 14, 2015, from http://www. goodreads.com/quotes/183589-things-work-out-best-for-those-who-make-the-best

Professional closers are fearless and ready to go out and speak with the customers. They don't have to be asked to do so.

**Communication skills.** Skilled closers are crystal clear in their communication, and they leave no room for ambiguousness. They paint pictures with their words, and they are great storytellers.

They are also listeners extraordinaire, and they hear between the lines. They are masters at discerning the true meaning of what is said and what is not said. They quickly understand the buyers' wants, needs, and hot buttons through questions.

They are well versed in a myriad of topics, and they can build rapport with a wide variety of clients whether it's someone on the top or the bottom of the economic scale, any race, breed, color, or religious background.

Top closers are also skilled at turning around standoffish or hostile clients. People in the car business tell me that I'm a great closer, but in actuality, I'm a great opener, and that is how I can close.

**Ability to overcome obstacles.** Many salespeople are scared of objections, but professional closers are not scared of those because they know these are the only things that stand between them and a sale. They thrive on hearing them, and they are great at helping the customers overcome them.

In the same way that closers are great at overcoming objections, they are also skilled at overcoming problems. Again, they pave the road to the sale by their leading questions.

They have an innate talent for thinking of a win-win compromise. Often times, the primary people you are selling a vehicle to, for example, a husband and wife or a parent and a son or daughter, don't agree because they don't have the same agenda. To find a win-win compromise is a great skill. In the car business, we talk about keeping the ball in the air. When the wife wants a four-runner, and the husband wants something bigger, they keep the ball in the air; they keep the discussion going until they find an option that everyone is happy with.

**Ability to set the right pace.** Gifted closers know when to build rapport, when to close, and when to ask for the order. Pace-setting the sale, switching the customers to their comfort speed, slowing down or speeding up as necessary, is another trait of a good closer. Many people's defense mechanism is to act like they are in a big hurry or have all the time in the world to make a decision, so being able to get the pace right is a wonderful trait.

If you have sales associates or managers who have half of these characteristics, they are far above the crowd. If they possess two-thirds of these, they are probably in the top 5% of sales associates you will ever encounter. They are rare eagles deserving of your time and attention.

A closer is like a star of a movie, and all the others in the movie are extras. The closer's movie looks the same every time. When someone watches a great closer in person, they get it. Many have never seen a great closer, so they have no way of understanding anything about them.

Many dealerships will hire teams of closers who travel around and do big promotional sales. I did that for several years. A lot of them are good closers. The downside is many of them are less than professional.

Professional, polished closers are better than a good general manager, salesperson, BDC clerk, or finance person. The people who have made it beyond their potential and are actual closers are very rare, and they are more precious than gold or diamonds.

Albert Einstein said, "Great spirits have always encountered violent opposition from mediocre minds."[20] People who don't understand closers give closers violent opposition. But closers make things happen, and that is the kind of people every dealer is looking for.

---

[20]   *Albert Einstein quote.* (n.d.). Retrieved December 14, 2015, from http://www. brainyquote.com/quotes/quotes/a/alberteins129798.html

John Maxwell, one of my favorite authors, said: "Value people. Praise effort. Reward performance."[21] I use this method with everyone. I even use a form of it with myself when I'm working. I don't give myself a reward until after the job is finished. When I approach a task or project, I give it my best. No matter what the results are, I have that clear conscience. Reward closers for acquiring more professional closing skills.

All too often, I have encountered clueless dealers or general managers who put no effort into growing their own closers. They will spend thousands of dollars on advertising to get customers to their dealership and on sign-on bonuses to recruit someone else's closers. However, someone else's closers probably left the place they were at because they were unhappy there, so when you recruit them, you play a losing game.

A want without a plan is simply wishful thinking. If you want to grow closers, you have to make a plan and then execute that plan.

---

[21] *Value people. Praise effort. Reward performance.* (n.d.). Retrieved December 14, 2015, from http://kindlequotes.tumblr.com/post/56124982620/value-people-praise-effort-reward-performance

# CHAPTER 11

# Words

When we were kids, we all heard the little rhyme "Sticks and stones may break my bones, but words will never hurt me." Nothing could be further from the truth. Words do hurt. They can also heal and help.

When you are in the sales industry, especially automotive sales, you don't have many toolboxes. Your main toolbox is your vocabulary – the words that you choose to use. How big of a word toolbox you have is up to you.

Say you hire a technician who is supposed to fix transmissions and motors, but the first day at work, this person shows up with a tiny $29 plastic tool set from Target or Walmart. Now, will you let this person work on motors and transmissions? I don't think so because he or she doesn't have the tools necessary to do the job. To be a good technician, you have to have a big toolbox full of useful tools. To be a successful salesperson, you need a big toolbox full of good tools as well.

Learning how to speak to people is imperative if you are going to be successful in this business. You also have to learn how to listen and not interrupt, how to lead the conversation, and how to ask closed or open-ended questions according to what you are trying to do.

You have to know how to open the deal through words and pictures that you paint with your words. These word pictures are unbelievably powerful because people can visualize them.

The words that you use are going to determine your wages. You have to have some product knowledge and good body language, appearance, and work ethic, but it largely comes down to your words. If you want to earn better wages, then use better words. Your words are going to be a direct reflection of what you make.

Regardless of your religious beliefs, I want you to be happy in your higher power. If you don't believe there is a higher power, maybe you believe you are the higher power. That is up to you, but I'm a Christian.

To the outside world, Christians who have chosen sales as a career must seem like a weird bunch. Christian salespeople struggle with life problems like everybody else. We just happen to believe that praying to our God in Jesus' name provides us with a divine direction. We believe that our worries and anxieties can be cast out to our God and that He takes care of some of these matters.

## A Biblical Perspective on Words

When I was learning to sell, I was searching for knowledge in the Bible. One day, I found the following verses about words in Proverbs:

Proverbs 6:2: "If you are snared in the words of your mouth, caught in the words of your mouth." (English Standard Version)

Proverbs 10:19: "When words are many, transgression is not lacking, but whoever restrains his lips is prudent."

Proverbs 10:20: "The words of the godly are like sterling silver; the heart of a fool is worthless." (New Living Translation)

Proverbs 11:12: "Whoever belittles his neighbors lacks sense, but a man of understanding remains silent." (English Standard Version)

Proverbs 12:18: "There is one whose rash words are like sword thrusts, but the tongue of the wise brings healing."

Proverbs 12:19: "Truthful lips endure forever, but a lying tongue is but for a moment."

Proverbs 12:25: "Anxiety in a man's heart weighs him down, but a good word makes him glad."

Proverbs 13:3: "Whoever guards his mouth preserves his life; he who opens wide his lips comes to ruin."

Proverbs 15:1: "A soft answer turns away wrath, but a harsh word stirs up anger."

Proverbs 15:2: "The tongue of the wise commends knowledge, but the mouths of fools pour out folly."

Proverbs 15:4: "A gentle tongue is a tree of life, but perverseness in it breaks the spirit."

Proverbs 15:23: "To make an apt answer is a joy to a man, and a word in season, how good it is!"

Proverbs 16:23: "The heart of the wise makes his speech judicious and adds persuasiveness to his list."

Proverbs 16:24: "Gracious words are like a honeycomb, sweetness to the soul and health to the body."

Proverbs 17:9: "Whoever covers an offense seeks love, but he who repeats a matter separates close friends." I think a lot of people repeat matters and separate close friends.

Proverbs 17:27: "Whoever restrains his words has knowledge, and he who has a cool spirit is a man of understanding."

Proverbs 17:28: "Even a fool who keeps silent is considered wise; when he closes his lips, he is deemed intelligent."

Proverbs 18:8: "The words of a whisperer are like delicious morsels; they go down into the inner parts of the body."

Proverbs 18:19: "A brother offended is more unyielding than a strong city, and quarreling is like the bars of a castle."

Proverbs 18:20: "People will be rewarded for what they say. They will be rewarded for how they speak." (New Century Version)

Proverbs 18:21: "Death and life are in the power of the tongue, and those who love it will eat its fruits." (English Standard Version)

Proverbs 18:23: "The poor beg for mercy, but the rich give rude answers." (New Century Version)

Proverbs 21:23: "Whoever keeps his mouth and his tongue keeps himself out of trouble." (English Standard Version)

Proverbs 25:11: "A word fitly spoken is like apples of gold in a setting of silver."

Proverbs 25:25: "Like cold water to a thirsty soul, so is good news from a far country."

Proverbs 26:20: "Without wood, a fire will go out, and without gossip, quarreling will stop." (New Century Version)

Proverbs 27:2: "Let another praise you, and not your own mouth; a stranger, and not your own lips." (English Standard Version)

Proverbs 29:20: "Do you see a man who is hasty in his words? There is more hope for a fool than for him."

Proverbs 30:32: "If you have been foolish, exalting yourself, or if you have been devising evil, put your hand on your mouth."

After having read these Scriptures, I thought about how many times my God kept telling me about the power of words. It was the opposite of "Sticks and stones may break my bones, but words will never hurt me." I don't think the Scriptures could have been clearer about the power of the words we choose. It's up to us to use better words. The Bible tells us if that we can be more persuasive if we use better words.

The passages from Proverbs ring loud and clear to me. When people go through droughts of not selling, and they have met the dreaded slump, or they say, "This isn't for me," then they are full of negative words. It's not limited to salespeople. Managers and dealers are often full of negative words as well.

You have to learn the words and the proper wording. Use that type of language, and use the right tone of inflection with every customer you meet on the car lot, especially with customers who are standoffish because they have been told for years that we are all shysters and gangsters and that we are going to steal their money.

## How to Speak with the Customers

Begin with a positive greeting when you welcome your customers to the dealership. A good conversation could go like this:

"Welcome to ABC Motors. My name is Roger. What are your names?"

"Our names are Clint and Misty."

"Hi Clint and Misty, are you here for our ___ sale today?" (The manufacturer or dealer is always having some kind of sale)

"No, we didn't know you were having a big sale today."

"Well, that's fantastic. You picked a great day to come out. As a matter of fact, we sent out over 40,000 emails and letters full of our specials. Hopefully, you got one."

"No, we didn't."

"That's okay. You can use mine. By the way, who is the lucky one? Who is getting a new car, truck, or van?"

If you start talking to the customers in that language, it doesn't fail you. Whenever you speak with a positive and calm demeanor, tone, and inflection, and you ask the right questions, it works.

Your words should first and foremost be positive. You cannot use negative words and put negativity into anything, and think that it will cause it to turn positive.

In the previous example dialogue, notice how I used the word "fantastic." It is an excellent word to use. If they ask you a question, for example: "What's the best price on that red F150?" say, "Fantastic! I'm glad you asked. Price is our specialty, and those F150s range from the low-20s to the mid-60s. By the way, what is it about that F150 that made you ask the price?"

"Great" is another powerful word. It puts people in a good mood.

The word "specialty" is also an effective one to use: "I'm glad you asked because here at ABC Motors, price is our specialty. Interest rate is our specialty. Finance is our specialty."

Other good phrases are "As you know" and "follow me." The last one is like a friendly command.

"Is that fair?" and "That's fair enough, isn't it?" and "Would that be fair?" are also excellent.

Other important phrases I use are "Tell me more," "Please tell me more," and "That's very interesting."

Use your words to instill in the customers a positive feeling about what you are showing them: "I believe you're really going to like this," or "I know you're going to love this," or phrase it as a question: "Don't you just love this?"

Whenever you are on a test drive, you can say, "Feel this," "Look at this," "Smell this," "Imagine this," "Listen to this," and "It's impressive, isn't it?" All these phrases are great.

Then there is a technique called "Feel, Felt, Found." Say someone comes in, and they have an issue or complaint, and they need help. Then you say: "I understand how you *feel*. I *felt* the same way until I *found* out." Whatever it is you found out, help them with the problem.

If you are going to disagree with somebody, then first tell them they are right: "You're absolutely right, however, ..." Then you can go into what you were going to say.

Tell people that they have made a "great decision" or an "excellent choice." It's true, so tell them; they "deserve it." People who have been working their whole lives driving junk cars deserve nice cars. Let them know that.

Always look for a better word to use whenever you are speaking with your customers. For example, instead of saying "down payment," you can say "initial investment," instead of "monthly payment," you can say "monthly investment," and instead of "your new car," say "your new vehicle" or "your new automobile."

People won't listen to you if you use a lot of slang. You need to level with your customers in terms of speech. There are different English accents all over the United States, and some people can barely understand each other. You need to be cognizant the different accents and be able to speak professionally with anyone.

## Asking and Listening

I have often trained salespeople who find it difficult to understand the power and importance of asking questions. It often comes down to that they want to tell somebody something. There is the old saying: "A wise man speaks because he has something to say, and a fool speaks because he has to say something." That is very true. Learning when to say something and when not to say something, and learning how to listen is very important.

When you do listen, there are certain powerful things that you need to learn how to say. Let me give some examples. First, use the word "share." Say a customer comes in and says: "I thought cars were cheaper in the town 50 miles from us." Then I will say: "Allow me to *share* this with you." "Share" is a word that makes people listen to you. It has a profound effect.

When I make phone calls to customers, let's call them Bob and Betty Buyer, I start the call saying: "Is this Bob and Betty Buyer? Typically, they answer "Yes," since I called their phone number. What I say next is this: "Great. What I have to say is important, but it's not urgent. Do you have a moment for me?" That is magic. It makes people say, "Gosh, I'm about to tee off on the eighth hole here, but yeah, hurry up," or "I'm about to walk in the store, but I've got a moment." They very rarely hang up on you; they are very rarely rude. "What I have to say is important but not urgent, do you have a moment for me?" It's magical, just like "Allow me to share something with you."

## Keep the Conversation Going

Your words can't put off sparks or push away or challenge people. If someone calls your dealership and asks: "Do you still have any red V6 automatics?" You can't just say "No," even if you don't have any. Continue by saying: "I don't see any out there right now. However, allow me to share this with you: We get a truckload or two almost every day, including some today. We probably have some coming in or that just came in. Please allow me to set an appointment with you at 10:45 tomorrow so I can show you all our colors." Or, "Allow me to share this with you: There are a couple of shades of red. I'd like to show you what the red ones look like in person. Can you make it out at 11 AM or 1 PM tomorrow?" Or "What is your second favorite color? Have you seen the new Deep Sea Blue? Do me a favor: Allow me to set an appointment with you at 11 AM or 1 PM to show you the colors. What works best for you?"

That is how you keep the conversation going. It amazes me how many times I hear salespeople who are otherwise sane and successful quickly cut off a conversation and leave it closed-ended. They will say something such as, "No, we don't have any of those." This leaves dead space in the conversation for the customers to cut off the communication.

## The 9 Square Grid

During a sales meeting a number of years ago, I learned about Paul D. Cummings' "9 Square Grid," which are nine things you should learn to say. Cummings calls it his customer-driven language pathway. The nine phrases are:

1. No Problem
2. Be Happy To
3. I Understand
4. Please Allow Me
5. I'm Confident
6. Easiest Part of My Job
7. Wouldn't Expect You To
8. Would You Do Me a Favor
9. Please Tell Me No[22]

---

[22]  Cummings, P.D. (2003) *How Many Different Ways Can You Use The 9 Square Grid?* [PDF document] Retrieved January 14, 2016, from http://assets.pdcwwe.com/pdf/9-SquareGrid-Toolkit.pdf

Those are nine amazing phrases that I always pass on to others. I like to give credit where credit is due whenever I learn something from someone, and I certainly learned something from Cummings with these particular phrases.

Several years ago, a couple of customers – a man and a woman – came to my lot, and the lady said that she had recently had back surgery and despite shopping all day, she couldn't find a car seat that was comfortable for her back.

At the time, we happened to have a line of cars that had seats that were designed by NASA. I had just read about it while taking my manufacturer certification test as the manager.

When the lady told me that she couldn't find a car that had seats that were comfortable for her back, I asked if she had driven one of those particular models. She said that she had just driven one and that it too had hurt her back.

Then I told her: "Well, in this particular model, the design of the seats has been derived from a design that NASA uses on their spaceships for comfort at speeds breaking the sound barrier and going in and out of our atmosphere. Please do me a favor; I want you to sit in this one and drive it."

We were talking about the same model of car that she had already driven. The only difference was that this was a larger version. Before she drove off, she warned me saying: "I think this is a waste of time. I don't believe any seats are comfortable enough for me."

When she came back from the test drive, she said in front of me and the sales associate: "I think that car made my back feel better." She had driven that model of car before she was aware of the NASA design. Once she was aware of it, it made her feel better about it, and she believed it made her back feel better.

There is nothing more powerful than the human mind. Until you believe that, it's not real to you. After you believe it, it is all that is real, and it works every day.

Every day, I say to myself that I'm going to be happy no matter what. Sometimes, I have to remind myself three or four times in a day that I am going to be in a good mood and be happy.

I am the person at my dealership who helps people handle upset customers. I am cautious not to raise my voice. I refrain from arguing with the customers. I allow them to speak, and I don't interrupt them, even when they repeat themselves, which they tend to do. I can be stern with an upset customer to keep things civil, but I am always polite.

I use Paul Cummings' words, and I tell them: "Please allow me to share something with you." I also use the "Feel, Felt, Found" technique, and I say: "I understand how you feel, I felt the same way until I found out___," which allows the customers to feel heard. Using proper verbiage calms down the customers and allows me to communicate with them.

If you arm yourself with better words, it makes you more powerful. With today's technology, you can just go online and find synonyms for the words that you currently use.

Practice using better words in your meet-and-greet, fact-finding, needs assessment, demonstration, presentation, objection overcoming, closes, and follow-up. Compile a list of words that you think may be better than the ones that you currently use. Better words mean better results.

Your level of eloquence and ability to put together sentences into questions or statements that excite your customers and make them listen to you are what will determine your wages. To change what you earn, you have to change what you say. You have to have great words to be a successful salesperson.

If you don't understand the power of words, consider this: You'll never speak like a pauper and be a prince.

The measure of salespeople is what it takes to discourage them. You will get discouraged a lot more quickly if you don't understand the power of words. If you don't understand how to use tone and inflection in your voice and exude excitement – over the phone and in person – then it will be very difficult for you.

There is nothing more important to learn than how to use your toolbox. You increase your toolbox in the manner you want to increase it. It can be as big or as little as you want it to be, but the bigger your toolbox is, the more you can speak with honey dripping from your lips, and the more you will sell.

To this day when I travel to dealerships all over the U.S. and Canada, I get on the phones and set appointments for sales people with live customers. They are always amazed. I work the sales floor talking to customers, and more often than not, I have the verbiage necessary to make the deal. My traffic driving strategies bring the traffic to pay for the training! Log onto to AutoMotiveCoach.net to schedule your LIVE EVENT TRAINING.

CHAPTER 12

# The Future Is Going to Be Here Whether We Are Prepared for It or Not

Currently, there are very good times in the auto industry. As far as new car sales are concerned, 2015 was awesome in terms of overall sales; 18 million is a lot of units!

With so many people buying cars, there is now a generation of car salespeople who are unfamiliar with how to do all the little things that make dealerships successful in any economy. Not only that, but we also have to be prepared for the modern times since things are changing.

There is a myriad of short-term fixes available to boost sales for a day or a week, such as traveling teams, advertising splurges, email blasts, mailers, and big spiffs. These create the kind of spikes you get from drinking energy drinks. Each time the caffeine wears off, you have less energy than you had before you drank the energy drink. Therefore, you need another energy drink and another one. Soon you need a more potent one. As they are loaded with caffeine, they are not healthy for your heart. There is no need to run your dealership in such a reckless and harmful manner. Why would someone run a multi-million-dollar dealership like a junkie? You wouldn't run your life that way. In your personal life, if you exercise daily and have proper nutrition, you will have much more energy than if you didn't. Is it so shocking that the same formula is what fuels a dealership to consistent highs?

Today's buyers are different than before, and that demands that you change your daily discipline. Habits are hard to form and even harder to change, but without changing your daily habits, the sustainable increases and high performances you desire will elude you. It seems too simple to be true, but professional improvement and optimal production are achieved through daily discipline and the things you do on a daily basis.

One of the measures of insanity is to do the same thing again and again and expect a different result. How long is it going to take you to make the necessary changes to accommodate modern buyers?

It is in your best interest to be prepared and ready. In this chapter, we will discuss 10 keys to selling in modern times, which will help you transition to this era before you are forced to so because your competition is doing it. This 10-step guide is specifically designed for capturing and converting the modern buyer, and it is guaranteed to make a positive impact on your dealership.

## 1. Start Each Day the Night Before

"Proper preparation prevents poor performance." That is something my old coach used to tell me, and it's very true. Many times when I come into dealerships, they are finishing up business from the day before.

The primary complaint customers have when it comes to buying a car is not the price negotiating, the selection, or the salespeople, but how much time it takes to buy the car. For that reason, the first thing you can do to accommodate today's buyer is ensuring that all the necessary ingredients for the day's business are in place already the night prior.

When you close the dealership for the night, check all the paper trays and printer cartridges and make sure that all the tools that are necessary to run the dealership seamlessly are in place. Leave no half-complete or unfinished business for the next day. Make sure that all the dealer trade packets are complete, all the CRM notes are in place, the tasks and functions are up to date, and the appointment board is full.

Let there be no units left out in your customer parking, and place all the vehicles where they are supposed to be. Make sure that they are ready to go and that drivers are lined up for any dealer trades you may have. Then, when the next day's opening shift walks in, the dealership is a machine ready to go.

## 2. Get in the Huddle

Each day, the opening managers, the finance and insurance managers, the business development center (BDC) representative, and sometimes even an office manager should gather up to discuss the following:

- How many appointments did we have yesterday?
- How many showed up?
- How many did we sell to?
- How many no-shows were there?
- How many people physically came to the lot?
- How many of them did we sell?
- How many test-drove?
- How far did they go?
- Which salesperson was with them?
- Which manager will call all the people who didn't show up or buy a car and all the people who did buy a car to congratulate them and make sure everything went well?
- How many appointments do we have for today?
- Who is confirming those appointments?
- What about the CITs (contracts in transit)?
- How can we save a deal?
- Who is not being productive and how can we help them?
- Are we on top of web monitoring and advertising?
- Who is doing the training today and what is the subject?
- What are we tracking?

Any other pertinent dealership news or information should also be discussed during these meetings. Prioritize all management sales and associate activities. Break everything down for each associate who needs a manager. Enter all the information in the CRM. Make sure that the CRM reflects everything that happened the day before. Don't let anything fall into the technology hole.

## 3. Get Managers on the Sales Floor

Back in the day, the customers would come to a car lot, meet a salesperson, and the salesperson would go back and forth between the customers and the manager four or five times before they agreed on a price of payment. Then, when they went to a finance manager, things could be completely different because the people at the desk could have been too lazy to pull the credit or they were so unprofessional that they just guessed what the interest rate or term could be. Those days of disrespecting the customers' time are gone.

The managers should be involved in the sales process from the meet-and-greet all the way to the follow-up. This way, the customers only meet a couple of people, and you eliminate steps in the process.

In the time to come, managers will take the initial contact from the customers via the Internet. Then they will set appointments, meet the customers, and sell the cars. They may be licensed to print the paperwork and do the financing as well. E-contracting has already swept the nation, and the old line printers are all but phased out.

Managed floors yield higher closing percentages, more gross, and more sales than unmanaged floors. Managing the sales tower is not as important as managing the sales floor. You don't need two, three, or four managers sitting in the sales tower waiting for salespeople to bring them deals. Never allow more than one manager in your sales tower unless he or she is swamped. Assign all the other managers to the floor to meet each customer face to face.

Having managers in charge of the sales process and the CRM from the floor will miraculously increase the up count – often double or triple it – and increase the closing percentage and your CSI (Customers Service Index).

We all know about the importance of logging each opportunity in the CRM. Assign managers to the floor with handheld devices such as smartphones or tablets that have your CRM downloaded on them. Instant access is the priority. This is not 1990 and 1990-style management.

Have your sales associates and managers use scripts, word tracks, and salesmanship to improve perceptually the tasks that they perform daily. Having several strong, active managers is the key.

The old-school way where associates went back and forth to the desk and finally got managers to get up and take a turnover is fading faster than cable TV. If your sales managers cannot sell, train, work the phone, and pretty soon do financing, then you have the wrong managers.

It's time to rely more on managers and less on sales associates. Most dealerships don't even comprehend the idea of training managers and having them involved in all aspects of the deal.

Since the average customer shops at fewer dealerships and drives fewer cars before purchasing, you have to get the managers involved. They can no longer just enjoy the comfort of the sales tower and avoid the customers. Those days are gone and will never come back again.

## 4. Never Send Your Customers to Shop or Refuse to Negotiate with an Uncommitted Buyer

Having a road to the sale or a step-by-step process is important, but it's not everything. Don't use it as an excuse to miss business, even if the process is broken down and the customers won't commit. Push, pull, or drag the deal through as many steps as possible using practiced and rehearsed negotiating techniques. That will stop a good percentage from shopping around. Don't create shoppers by over-enforcing a process. The rule of thumb is that you should use your process every time the customers allow you to.

If the play breaks down, you should scramble and still run a play. Take each deal as far as you can. Don't miss deals for the process, and don't break the process unless you are forced to do so.

If customers don't want to test drive or follow certain steps of the sale, don't say: "Well, get your best number at another store, bring it back here, and we will match it or beat it." Instead, give them your best deal upfront. Never send your customers to shop. Your odds of closing the deal with them right then are a lot better than they are ever going to be because they likely won't come back.

## 5. Have Mandatory Daily 20-Minute Sales Training

These daily meetings should take place upon the arrival of the second shift. They are planned and should last no longer than 20 minutes.

Each session is training on subjects that are designed to improve selling skills, negotiating techniques, phone skills, etc. The "Twenty-Five Sales Meetings" in the Appendix of this book are, as the title indicates, 25 sales meetings you can have with your associates. I highly recommend role-play in each session. The goal of the training is a perpetual improvement, which is paramount.

The training should happen every day. It's just like taking a shower. If you don't take a shower every day, you start to stink. If you don't train every day, you start to stink. Managers must improve, perform, or attend this training every day. The only people who are excused are the ones who are working on a live deal with a customer.

## 6. Create Efficient Structures

Nowadays, some restaurants allow you to swipe your card at your table, so you don't have to stand at a register or wait for the waiter or waitress. And some stores have self-checkouts for quick exits.

No one wants to wait to give you money, especially if it's $40,000 or $100,000.

It is unacceptable to make customers wait hours for a finance manager or send them home and ask them to come back the next day to finish up. It's time to redefine and reevaluate each of the traditional manager's functions and how we value customers' time.

The time of having one person who closes deals, one person who submits deals, one who desks deals, one who does the contract, and one who does finance and insurance is soon to be extinct – just like the dinosaurs. Having managers who are well versed in submitting deals, e-contracting, selling a product, maximizing the back end, deal structures, selling the vehicle, and helping people check out more quickly will separate you from the dinosaurs.

A busy-buyer program where you contract the sale offsite by picking up the trade and delivering the new unit to the customers' house is another thing that will separate you from the dinosaurs.

You probably think: "Oh gosh, this means changing the way we do business." Change is scary, but changing the way we do things and the way we think to improve old methods that stink is the only thing that makes any sense. Don't be stuck in the past or afraid of change because the cost of doing nothing will soon exceed the cost of changing.

## 7. Manage All Departments

Manage the BDC, the e-commerce department, and the Internet department, and bridge the gap between these departments.

Having sales managers strategically price the units, assist in appointment setting, follow up with the leads, and send emails and text messages is the key. Leaving the leads entirely in the hands of the BDC or the sales staff is not nearly as productive as when managers actually manage the BDC, the e-commerce department, and the Internet department, and interact with the customers. It's better if the sales managers manage the interaction via email, phone, text messages, etc., and every incoming call and email goes through quality control by the general manager or the general sales manager.

If your general manager or general sales manager isn't listening to the incoming calls and reviewing the emails on a regular basis, then why aren't they? A high percentage of your customers are contacting you via email or phone before setting foot in the dealership, so it's common sense that the top-level managers should be involved with every contact with both hands.

I strongly recommend implementing a pricing strategy where all prices are uniform on all areas of the Internet. This provides credibility. No matter if you use a one-price strategy, a starting-point strategy, or any other form of pricing strategy, make sure that it's uniform and management driven.

## 8. Manage the Time Bandit Known as the Internet

Social media, YouTube, ESPN, news sites, porn sites, and the like steal man-hours from every dealership. What is easier to distract? A cat with a red laser light pen or a sales person with the Internet?

Every activity that the associates perform and every minute of the day should be in your CRM. You can manage and monitor them by printing them out and going over them.

Having one manager assigned to a sales desk and the remaining managers assigned to the sales floor and the lot will alleviate a lot of the Internet surfing. Blocking the sites above is another good idea.

Monitoring each sales associate and manager's daily activities, training, lot parties, merchandising, CRM management, BDC management, follow-up, and face-to-face customer interaction is the best way to elude this time bandit.

## 9. Have Mandatory Training for Sales Managers and BDC Representatives

After all this change that I have asked you to implement, I implore you never to get away from mastering the art of salesmanship. Very few invest in manager training. Instead, it is common to overspend on manager turnover or advertising to offset poor performance. Daily BDC representative training is currently only performed by true curve setters.

I dare you to listen to today's sales calls and print copies of every email that is sent from the dealership. Get blind copied on each of them. It will wake up and perhaps scare you.

The reality is that in this modern time of selling, becoming better at the art of selling is ignored. But there are selling tips, techniques, and verbiage that are time-tested and proven to be effective, and they should be practiced, studied, and perfected. There is a lot to learn about the intricacies of selling, body language, non-verbal communication, when to ask, when to be quiet, tone, attitude, time management, coaching, opening a deal, closing a deal, and so on.

What if a professional sports team didn't insist that the coaches and team captains attend practice, study, and train every day? Since there is so much to learn, everyone needs to train every day. When your people improve, results improve. No one is too good to learn.

## 10) Coach

You must have coaches employed in your management roles. Everyone who knows me knows how important I believe coaching is to team building. I won't elaborate on coaching here since I have already talked about it a lot, but the bottom line is if you don't have coaches who are improving and adding value to your managers and sales associates, you are missing the boat on how important it is to achieve what can be achieved.

These are 10 things that have to be done because it is the evolution of the car business whether you like it or not. There were people who rode horses who said: "I'll never get one of those motor cars. They require gas, and they break down, so I don't want one. I can get on my horse and go anywhere I want." Don't have that attitude toward your dealership.

# Don't Take Selling out of the Equation

As the times change, we have to be wary of those who attempt to take selling out of the equation. In the past two and a half decades that I can speak for, it has been very popular for trainers and manufacturers to attempt to do just that.

I can remember when a certain auto manufacturer bought all the dealerships in inner-city Tulsa and Oklahoma City and called them the "Auto Collection". They convinced themselves that we, the people in retail were bad guys and didn't know what we were doing. They were going to show us. So they didn't want to hire car salespeople and managers with experience.

They went to one price shopping since they belived people "hated" negotiating. It didn't work out so well. Some of the other manufacturers bought some dealerships in other states, and it didn't work out so well there either. They went to one price shopping and sales plummeted. Soon they were running ads begging people with sales skills and management skills to work for them.

I also remember when Car Max and Auto Nation first got started. They appraised cars and handed out tickets for what cars were worth, had one price shopping. They bought huge facilities. Everybody wanted to take selling out of the equation. Eventually everyone wastes tons of money only to learn the customers will search for a better deal if all you are doing is selling to their logic. Logic has no place in love and auto sales.

The big secret they never understood is that everyone wants to feel special, and everyone wants to feel good about the deal. A deal that everyone can get doesn't make anyone feel as good. Why is that so difficult to digest?

It may work at Target or Walmart, but on a big-ticket item like a house or a car, people need that feel good, and they were not getting that. That was the salesmanship many wanted to take out of the equation. They falsely claimed that we ought to tiptoe around the customers and hope that the customers would volunteer to buy a car after a great demonstration and maybe one weak attempt at closing.

I strongly disagree with that. Most of the customers I make deals with to this day say, "I was not prepared to buy a car today" or "I was not going to buy a car today" as they take delivery of their new car. Even in today's information age, the percentage of customers who fall into this category is still very high.

A professional might be able to close the deal without a trial close, but that won't work for all customers. You will miss 20% to 25% of your business if you don't know how or when to use trial closes and selling techniques.

It's not wise to take the selling out of sales. I strongly suggest building value, earning the right to ask, and understanding the customers' body language before asking. Remember: A deal must be open before it can close.

If you see that the deal is open, then ask the tough questions. Taking the tough questions out of the process will leave you with a lower closing percentage and a lot of promises that end badly.

The skill of asking the tough questions without offending is what trainers should be teaching. The objections are supposed to come out sooner or later, and they are not going to come forward unless you ask. They are not deal killers or roadblocks as you may think; they are road maps to the sale.

All pros know the verbiage to take the pressure off the customers. We discussed this in a previous chapter. With the right verbiage, you can keep pushing the deal to the next step, and if you have made the value exceed the price, you can close.

Buying decisions are 80% emotion and 20% logic. They always have been, and they always will be, despite the millions and maybe even billions of dollars that have been spent in an attempt to refute or reverse this phenomenon.

Emotion is defined as an "Instinctive or intuitive feeling,"[23] "deriving from one's circumstances, mood, or relationship with others."[24] Logic is defined as "reasoning conducted or assessed according to strict principles of validity."[25] Two things logic is foreign to, SALES and LOVE. Being armed with this knowledge causes an all too real pain inside each of us as sales professionals because we often get so focused on the logical aspect of the sale that we ignore the emotional aspect of it. How could we be so blind that we ignore this magical aspect of the selling process when we go through it every day? The secret to selling is so secret that we forget it ourselves, and we get jaded and forget that we have to put the magic in the deal.

I hear salespeople and managers say that customers are dumb if they don't take the deal they are offered. Well, let's review that. Did the salespeople do a whole-hearted test drive? Did they assess the customers' needs? Did they build rapport? Did they follow the steps to the sale? Or did they go straight to the numbers – the logic side? If you go through the process the wrong way and expect it to produce the same result as when it is done the right way, then who is the idiot? Be focused on the 80% rather than the 20%.

When we don't do it the right way, we travel a difficult road, and we butcher deals. The customers lose all faith in us, and we convert buying customers into shoppers.

There are managers who do not get involved in deals. They want to claim that they are the ultimate authority, and they choose to avoid customers for this reason. The reality is they choose to avoid the selling effort because they have experienced the pain of

---

[23]   Emotion [Def. 1.1]. (n.d.). *Oxford Dictionaries Online*. Retrived December 14, 2015, from http://www.oxforddictionaries.com/definition/english/emotion

[24]   Ibid.

[25]   Logic [Def. 1]. (n.d.). *Oxford Dictionaries Online*. Retrived December 14, 2015, from http://www.oxforddictionaries.com/definition/english/logic

skipping the process, and they butcher deals by getting right down to the logic.

How do we achieve optimum communication with our customers and keep in mind their intuitive, instinctive feeling that is derived from circumstances, moods, or relationships with us? We let them know what we are supposed to let them know without skipping the steps to the sale. The people at the top cannot skip the steps. A lot of times, these people don't even understand these steps. Then they wonder why their associates can't do them.

Now in the technology era, we tend to complain and ask: "Where is the gross? How can I make money in this era?" I have traveled to 41 states in the United States and six provinces in Canada, and everywhere I went, the dealers would say something like: "In our community, we have a competitor that advertises cars for $2,000 net losses, and we can't compete with that." Now it's the Internet. The dealers say: "In our community, we have all these corporate-owned dealerships that are driving away all the mom-and-pop dealerships, and they're advertising net losers, and there is just no gross on deals anymore." It's simply not true; you can do well in any market.

We can't skip the processes, techniques, and systems that are designed to discover the customers' wants, needs, and objections so that we can go down the road of the sale, and then wonder why the customers won't buy the cars.

As times change, and we evolve into having to respect the customers' time more, it's more important that we understand that emotions are an intuitive, instinctive feeling deriving from one's circumstances, moods, or relationship with others. That is putting the magic into sales.

# Final Words

As the business, our customer base, and the buying process rapidly change, there is a lot we have to open our minds to. We have to look forward, not in the rearview mirror.

It has been my honor to be able to share this book with you, and I hope it has been helpful to you. However, all the literature in the world won't you help you unless you implement it.

I have a lot more information that I would like to share with you. If you are interested in improving, I'm glad to help. You can visit my website, automotivecoach.net, or you can visit me on Facebook, AutomotiveCoach sales training, or you can follow me on twitter @AutoCoach30.

If you want traffic and results why gamble with your ad dollars? My methods are proven. Log on to AutoMotiveCoach.net to schedule your live Event training with Roger TODAY!

# Appendix

# Day Planner

| Date | | | |
|---|---|---|---|
| 7:00:00 | | 1. _____ | |
| | | 2. _____ | |
| 8:00:00 | | 3. _____ | |
| | | 4. _____ | |
| 9:00:00 | | 5. _____ | |
| 10:00:00 | | | |
| 11:00:00 | | Notes: _____ | |
| 12:00:00 | | | |
| 13:00:00 | | | |
| 14:00:00 | | | |
| 15:00:00 | | *Commit your work to the lord, and your plans will be established.* | |
| 16:00:00 | | *~Proverbs 16:3* | |
| 17:00:00 | | *Many are the plans in a man's heart, but it is the LORD'S purpose that prevails.* | |
| 18:00:00 | | | |
| 19:00:00 | | *~Proverbs 19:21* | |
| 20:00:00 | | | |

# Twenty-Five Sales Meetings

The 25 sales meetings in this chapter are based on the content of the main part of the book. These meetings will help everyone understand what to do and what our purpose is, and they will help everyone move in the same direction. A crew of people going in the same direction is a very powerful thing.

Everything in these 25 meetings will make you a professional. They will take you from success to significant. Without knowing these, you won't be as effective as you could be.

Every sales manager, finance manager, salesperson –everybody in the sales department needs to know these 25 20-minute sales meetings frontward, backward, and sideways.

## 1. The Sales Cycle

Every person who is employed in the sales industry from dealers to general managers to first-day sales associates is somewhere in the sales cycle. Learn each stage, and come full circle.

Everyone begins at Stage 1, the wonderful world of being green! Then you matriculate on to Stage 2, the dark stage, where 80% of associates do not make it out with their job. Then some light shines on you, and you move forward out of the darkness.

If you are able to reach Stage 3, you have an 80% chance of being a lifer in the sales industry. Stage 3 is where you learn how to "do it yourself." While you can do it yourself, you are not a person who is in tune to uplift others; it's all about you. But you earn professional wages, and you are good at your job.

Stage 4 is reserved for the rare eagles who can do it themselves and lift up the entire team with inspiration, assistance, and sharing of knowledge. They have a positive attitude that permeates throughout. This life wheel is a fluid situation, not a permanent address, so always be cognizant of where you are.

## 2. The Seven Steps to the Sale

Following the steps to the sale is key, and you must chart, track, study, and improve. If you do not understand the importance of following a planned-out sales process, it is likely that you live in a very unstable sales world. Highs and lows, peaks and valleys are much more than ordinary.

Each step is to be taken seriously and discussed in detail. CRM allows us to chart ups, test drives, proposals, closes, T.O.s, etc. If you can see where you are getting weak, you can focus on the weak area and fix it. The goal is a perpetual improvement.

## 3. Questions Are the Answer

Learn how and when to ask quality questions, and what questions to ask. Questions are the answer. In the Bible, Jesus asked more than 300 questions. Why? He did it because questions lead to the answer. The more you get prospects to tell you about themselves, their wants, their needs, their desires, their fears, their goals, etc., the more likely you are to make a sale. K-E-Y – knowledge empowers you. Customers do not care how much you know until they know how much you care. Stop trying to tell your way to the sale. Start asking your way, and you will see a vast improvement in sales. Answer questions. For example, if a customer asks: "What is the bottom dollar on that red F-150?" you answer: "Those F150s typically run from low teens up to $70,000 plus. What is it about that F150 that spurred you to ask the price?"

## 4. An Appointment Culture

Learn the four types of calls and how to make them. Discuss the power of phone skills. Each appointment set is over one-third of a car sold. As a rule of thumb, 75% of the appointments will show, and of those, 50% will sell. If my math is right, that means 37.5% of manager-verified appointments result in deliveries.

Incoming calls will cause salespeople to fight over the phone, yet these same salespeople are allergic to outgoing calls. There are incoming calls, and then there are three types of outgoing calls: sold follow-up, unsold showroom traffic, and prospecting. Being efficient on the phones is a sure way to appointments. We have already established that appointments lead directly to sales. A dealership that is not setting appointments is a dealership surfing on a wave they did not create.

Creating traffic by calling and setting appointments is a skill that keeps the sales momentum going. Mining the service department and calling orphan owners and orphan unsold showroom traffic is essential because there are many customers waiting to hear from us!

## 5. Your Pie

It's about fixing the person before you can fix the salesperson – getting your life and your mind right.

Your mind is your "pie," and the object of the game is to keep flies out of your pie. Staying focused is more difficult than you may realize. With bills, kids, extracurricular activities, and life in general, there are a lot of things that can consume your mind when you are supposed to be working. How do you keep your problems at the curb rather than bringing them into the dealership?

If you spend more time talking to other salespeople than you do customers, you have a prioritizing issue and a production issue. Attempting to sell cars with your life out of balance is like driving a car with flat spots on the tires; it's a bumpy and uncomfortable ride. Learn to balance your time and your life, prioritize the important things and focus on the task at hand, *every day.*

# 6. Handling Rejection

Learn to be fueled by failures and defined by your victories. Become a human conduit ingesting negative and putting out positive.

At times, customers will lie and be unruly, illogical, demanding, and overbearing. Do not take it personally, and do not become angry or standoffish or try to set them straight. If you start a debate, you lose a deal.

One of the reasons you earn professional wages is that you understand human nature and the flawed behavior and attitude of many people. You accept the poor behavior, and in return, you kill them with kindness and professionalism.

Never get mad at your money. Never get down because of a deal or several deals. Always stay on the high road, the "principle of path." We will arrive at our destination if we keep focused and move forward without stopping or veering off course. You didn't make the world this way; it was this way when you got here. However, if you want to change the world, do it by being kind and courteous with never ending professionalism, honesty, and integrity.

# 7. Customer Service

Taking care of people is the difference between a career and a job. Nice always wins. Go above and beyond. Under-promise and over-deliver. Smile. Follow the 10-foot rule. Open doors and return phone calls. Respect your customers and their time. Help people who are not your customers, the ones you have not made a dime on, because it's the right thing to do.

A world-class customer service experience will separate you from the competition in a positive manner. People won't buy just because you are overly nice; you still have to ask for the order. But it sure raises your odds and, in the long run, customers will run back to you. Turn pro and treat people how you would like to be treated.

## 8. Negotiating

Present the numbers like a professional. Learn what to say, when to say it, how to say it, and when to *shut up*.

Knowing how to negotiate properly is a highly profitable skill to add to your repertoire. I see customers out-negotiate salespeople in dealerships every day, and it is scary. The old "I will drop the price and give you more for your trade until you buy" is not a close. There are many intricacies to winning in negotiations, and sales managers and sales associates are crazy *not* to practice the best techniques, especially in a situation such as when you present the numbers, and you have the same objections to overcome day in and day out.

## 9. The T.O.

Learn how to give and take a T.O. properly, and learn why it will make or break you. The boss must talk, or everyone's money walks.

The art of the T.O. is a many-splendored thing. When it is properly executed, it is both efficient and profitable. However, when it is performed by poorly prepared or untrained personnel, it is neither efficient nor profitable.

This aspect of the deal must be practiced, drilled, and rehearsed to the 10th degree at every dealership. It must be role-played, scripted, and perfected. Managers often complain that their salespeople need training when it is the managers who need the training.

## 10. K-E-Y – Knowledge Empowers You!

Get paid what you are worth! Sales is the one place that does not care about age, race, gender, socioeconomic status, background, or education. What you earn is what you are worth. There should be no excuses, finger pointing, or victims.

If you want a raise, then learn more and study. When you know better, you do better. Learn and then learn some more! Read or listen to books by Zig Ziglar, Jim Zeigler, Jackie Cooper, Joe Verde, Grant Cardone, Dave Anderson, or some of the many sources of knowledge. Join a social media site. Even the manufacturers have quality sales knowledge these days.

If you are green, you are growing, and if you are ripe, you are rotting! The auto sales business is always changing, but the wisdom of selling techniques last forever.

## 11. Relaxing and Persuasive Verbiage

Learn phrases and word tracts to assist your persuasiveness. A bigger word toolbox and better language produces a better paycheck.

The words we use can cause the customers' body language to improve or to clench up. We need to know what words and phrases to use to relax the customers. Why would salespeople *not* want to know the most proficient words to say to customers? Certain words and phrases are more pleasing to the ear and, as a result, more efficient to the sales process.

## 12. Coaching

Teamwork makes the dream work. Helping others will propel you while making the team better makes you better. There is no room for the greedy fish.

Coaching is the most important of all processes. You need to be focused for perpetual improvement to happen; it is not just going to take care of itself. Being the wind beneath someone's wings and having someone in your corner to help you see what you can't see is essential. Have a team atmosphere and do things as a team. None of us can do what all of us can do. Team-first attitudes are caught as often as they are taught. It all starts with the leadership of the dealership.

## 13. Getting out of and Avoiding Slumps

We will face slumps early and often, and it's all about how we deal with them effectively. There is no such thing as a salesperson who does not face the dreaded slumps from time to time. The best practices to avoid them and overcome them are to be taught on a regular basis.

## 14. Prospecting, Networking, and Self-Marketing

Create your brand and stay active. Idle time is the devil's playtime.

In an ever-changing business, we have to keep pace with the times. Marketing yourself is key in today's age. Everyone wants more traffic, social media, and e-commerce, and there are many ways of reaching the public.

Idle time has to be replaced with work. Spend time sending emails, texts, cards, and videos to customers. Just as idleness will stymie sales, activity will yield results. Always do your best and give the extra effort because it always pays off. Laziness, on the other hand, doesn't pay very well.

## 15. Body Language

Learn both reading and dictating body language. Customers tell you everything without saying anything.

Who knew that the laws of attraction exist? All the little things like hand clenching, leg crossing, hands in the pockets, and lack of eye contact are very important. Smiling, covering the mouth, fidgeting, and crossing of the arms or legs tell you everything without a word. There are many things to learn about body language, and learning them takes, time, effort, energy, and practice.

## 16. Expert Listening

Listen between the lines and try to understand what the customers really mean. Listen with an open mind. Don't interrupt or argue. Listen so intently that the customers can't ignore you.

Especially during Stage 2, it is very difficult for salespeople to listen to clients.

Words often have a much different meaning than what is on the surface, so learn to listen. Listening is a true skill, and it will pay dividends if you master the art.

## 17. Top Opening and Closing Techniques

Nothing can close before is has opened, so learn how to recognize and pounce on an open deal and close it.

If you want to be a great closer, you must become a great opener. Know how to get the customers' body language right before asking for the order. Learn the most productive responses to the most common objections. There is no excuse for not learning to be a great opener and a great closer! Don't be lazy. Learn these techniques today!

## 18. Markup/Negotiations

Profit is not a dirty word. Don't be ashamed to make a profit. The average markup at any retail establishment is considerably higher than the markup on automobiles. Walmart, The Dollar Store, and Target all have significantly more markup than any new car on the market. The average markup on a car is very small. In most cases, it is 4% to 8%. Furniture, jewelry, appliances, and clothing retailers have many times more markups than car lots. There is no reason to be ashamed to ask for a fair profit.

## 19. Green Enthusiasm Versus Experienced Indifference (Elephant Meeting)

Your attitude determines your altitude. Don't be a know-it-all. Instead, be a share-it-all. The salesperson who no longer listens in meetings and is no longer learning is a salesperson who is soon to be passed up by the up-and-comers.

Do not be a sourpuss or a negative Nancy dragging down other people. Gravediggers eventually fall into the pits they dig, so *don't* be a gravedigger. If you don't have something positive to say, keep it to yourself or share it in private with the person whom it concerns.

Don't gossip, or the gossip will come back on you! No one cares how many cars you used to sell, how great some other dealership is, or how great the good old days were. Have the enthusiasm of a green pea and keep your attitude in check. The negative people are often the last ones to know they are dragging down everyone else. Be positive, helpful, and enthusiastic. Enthusiasm is such an extraordinarily large piece of the synergistic selling road to success.

## 20. Overcoming Common Objections

Learn the best practices for overcoming the most common objections you face via the web, in person, or on the phone. Practicing overcoming the basic objections we face every day only makes common sense. The idea that millions of dollars of commission monies are squandered to the same objections every day is insane to me. While the same basic objections are huge stumbling blocks in the road for amateurs, professionals practice, drill, and rehearse the top objection overcoming materials so that they can make the commissions that the amateurs miss.

## 21. Sales Forecasting Done Right

Make a plan and work accordingly. Prioritize and do your due diligence *every day.*

Every month begins with a forecast and a work plan. Stick to the plan. Do not be like a ship at sea with no motor or rudder, just being blown all around. Prioritize your day, week, month, and year. Letting unimportant things consume your time and leaving little time for important things is not smart. Tracking everything you do allows you to improve.

## 22. Look at and Listen to Yourself

Do you look and dress like a million bucks? Are you well groomed and sharp looking? Do you look like a pro? Is your shirt wrinkled? Is your hair unkempt? You will be surprised what a professional appearance will do for you. Have you listened to yourself? Most people are surprised when they begin recording themselves.

## 23. Habits of Pros Versus Habits of Joes

Winning is in the little things. The daily habits are what separate the winners from the losers. What are your daily habits? What habits do you have that you need to lose? What habits do you need to incorporate into your day?

## 24. Eagles Versus Turkeys

Build your support group and find out how to gain inspiration and be supportive of others while avoiding gravediggers! We get by with a little help from our successful friends.

We all have mentors who have helped us. Having a successful and positive influence is a great boost to salespeople. Soar by yourself at work rather than congregate. Be supportive of others but not dragged into the huddles and complaining. The Research and Development Committee is no place to make a good living. Do not hang with the turkeys when they peck poop and huddle up. While the eagles fly above storms, the turkeys get rained on and sometimes look up and drown themselves. Be an eagle.

## 25. Closers

Closers are highly productive salespeople who know about asking for the order and how to get it! The difference between closer and loser is a C, which stands for *can*. The closer can because they believe they can.

Customers don't buy what you sell; they buy what you believe. The great openers are halfway there to being great closers. Learning the *how to*'s of being a great closer are what separates the contenders from the pretenders. Learning how to become a top-notch closer is paramount to being a highly compensated consummate professional.

# About the Author

Roger Williams has been in the car industry for two and a half decades, and he is an industry expert.

He grew up in rural Oklahoma, about an hour southeast of Oklahoma City. No one's life is perfect, and neither was Roger's. His grandparents raised him in a very modest, old home. His best friend since he can remember is his cousin, Reverend Jeff Nance. They are very close in age, and they grew and up more like brothers.

In his early years, Roger tended to his granddad's goats, chickens, and even coon dogs, which they raised and sold. They grew corn, squash, tomatoes, onions, melons, and okra. As a kid, Roger enjoyed plowing the field with his granddad.

As a schoolboy, Roger loved playing sports with his friends, and that passion continues today. He has played semi-pro football and scrimmaged with a professional basketball team. Roger's backyard served as a boxing ring for many years, and the matches would often be very competitive. This competitiveness carried over into sales; a world Roger entered in the early 1990s. Roger was a member of Lynn Hickey Dodge's World Record 2,813 retail units.in a single month

Beginning as a salesperson, Roger quickly worked his way up the ranks, and those "in the know" recognize him as a specialist in coaching , training, dealership turnaround, team building .As an elite performer at all levels of dealership operations, Roger has a true gift for inspiring teams to greater achievement.

Roger has performed in 41 of the 50 United States and six Canadian provinces in roles such as speaker, trainer, consultant, or under management contract. As a real "been there, done that" kind of fellow, his repeated and prolonged success is directly tied to the energy, enthusiasm, and positive attitude Roger brings. He doesn't just talk about it, he does it. He speaks and trains with passion every day. His attitude is very rare and even more contagious. He has a true gift for inspiring and teaching dealers, salespeople and managers, using a real-world approach that is as unique as it is fun. This gift has earned Roger the moniker "The AutoMotiveCoach."

Roger and Lori reside in Joplin, Mo. Where Lori is an interior decorator. They are crazy dog people, with between 5 and 7 dogs most of the time. Imperfect christians who believe we all need a close personal relationship with God.

To learn more about Roger or book him for a speaking engagement or for your own live training session, go to
www.Automotivecoach.net
Email address: Automotivecoach@gmail.com
Twitter handle: @AutoCoach30
Facebook: AutomotiveCoach Sales training blogs

Made in the USA
Middletown, DE
10 October 2022

12440199R00106